£2-50

MY WAY

MY WAY

by

Glenn Turner

HODDER AND STOUGHTON
AUCKLAND LONDON SYDNEY TORONTO

To Billy Ibadulla

FOREWORD by TOM GRAVENEY

It is with great pleasure that I write this foreword to Glenn's excellent book.

I first saw Glenn in the nets at Worcester, after I had been told how useful a player he was by Billy Ibadulla, and it only required him to play two or three shots to confirm that here was a young man with more talent than most; and Worcestershire had the chance to sign him.

A few years later I was at the wicket with him when he broke a Worcester record by scoring his tenth century of the season – a truly wonderful performance. When Glenn commenced first-class cricket he was terribly slow and I was told by many people – players and spectators alike – that he was jeopardising our chances of winning games by staying in! How they have had to eat their words. The hardest thing to do when one begins to play first-class cricket is to occupy the crease for a period of time. How well I recall my own start, over twenty innings for about two hundred runs – not very good!! This was Glenn's reason for being slow. He did not want to make any mistakes and on some occasions he did make winning a match rather difficult for the other ten players concerned. However, as his captain, I was able to appreciate this as being part of his apprenticeship to "big" cricket.

The turning point came in a Sunday League match against Essex. After being left to score something like 235 to win, Worcester were 7 for 0 after seven overs, Glenn 0 not out. Obviously, something drastic had to happen and in the next six overs he completed his own 50. From then on I think he realised that shots could be played safely over the heads of fielders and he has never looked back.

Glenn is an excellent example to budding young cricketers. He is one of the few players in the game who picks up his bat straight and brings it down the same way. He does the basic things in batting correctly which make run getting so much easier.

When I left for Australia in 1970 – the season Glenn scored his ten centuries – I said that Glenn Turner would be the batsman of the Seventies. Since returning I have not seen anything to alter my opinion. Good luck to a fine player.

Contents

Chapter		page
1	Beginnings	15
2	A Contract with Worcestershire	29
3	Playing for New Zealand	33
4	On Tour in India, 1969	43
5	New Zealand v. Pakistan, 1969–70	57
6	New Zealand Tour of the West Indies, 1972	65
7	English County Cricket	85
8	Limited-overs and First-class Cricket in England	89
9	The Benefits of Sponsorship	99
10	Marriage	105
11	Short Tours: Cricket for Fun	111
12	My Approach to Batting	121
13	Playing Spin Bowling	137
14	1,000 Runs by the End of May	151
15	Victory over Australia, 1974	159
	For the Record	187

Illustrations

between pages 32 and 33

Glenn Turner: a 1974 portrait[1]
Four former captains of Otago Boys High School firstXI[2]
Turner is given out lbw to Peter Parfitt, Wellington 1966[3]

between pages 48 and 49

Don Kenyon making his last appearance at New Road with Turner as junior partner[4]
The first test at Lord's, 1969: Boycott is caught by Turner[5]
Hendricks watches as Turner drives square to the boundary[6]
Turner about to catch Gavaskar, Bombay, 1969[7] ´

between pages 96 and 97

Turner walks off the field after carrying his bat through the second innings of the first test at Lord's, 1969[5]
Murray appeals for a catch but Turner survives[5]
A batsman in full command: Turner's 153 for New Zealand against the M.C.C. at Lord's, 1973 (upper photos[8], lower[5])
Colin Cowdrey at the completion of a cover drive[5]
Tom Graveney driving a wide delivery from Johnny Gleeson[5]

between pages 112 and 113

Dressing room scene during New Zealand's match against President's XI, Montego Bay, 1972
Turner brings his total to over 1000 runs before the end of May, 1973[8], and celebrates afterwards with fellow New Zealanders

A narrow escape: Turner batting during the second test against Australia, Christchurch 1974[9]
The dismissal of Greg Chappell that brought the Lancaster Park crowd to its feet[9]
Turner plays a controlled shot during the second test, Christchurch, 1974[9]
Young supporters race to congratulate Turner on the first of his two centuries in the second test at Christchurch, 1974[9]
Glenn Turner and Dick Motz celebrate the defeat of Australia at Lancaster Park, 1974[9]
John Parker, Sukhinder and Glenn[10]

between pages 160 and 161

Glenn plays his "slash"[6]
All balance and concentration[6]
Champagne shower for the Worcestershire captain, Norman Gifford to celebrate winning the county championship[6]

between pages 176 and 177

Worcestershire county champions, 1974[6]
Khalid "Billy" Ibadulla[6]
Glenn Turner bowling[6]

Grateful thanks are due to the following, whose photographs are reproduced in this book:
[1]Morris Kershaw, F.N.Z.P.P.A., A.R.P.S., A.I.B.P.; [2]*Wanganui Chronicle*; [3]Photo News, Wellington; [4]Berrows Newspapers, Worcester; [5]Sport and General; [6]Ken Kelly and the *Birmingham Evening Mail*; [7]Saby Fernandes; [8]Patrick Eagar; [9]*Christchurch Press*; [10]Neville Chadwick.

Acknowledgments

I would particularly like to acknowledge the help and assistance of the following friends and associates: Dick Brittenden and Ray Cairns for compiling statistics and helping with the selection of photographs; Frank A. Green and Ian Walter for run charts; Morris Kershaw FNZPPA, ARPS, AIPB, Patrick Eagar, Ken Kelly and *The Press*, Christchurch for permission to use photographs; Tom Graveney for kindly consenting to write a foreword; Anne-Marie Tobin for her typing assistance; Des Woods and *The Press*; Sukhi, my wife, for her typing and being my biggest distraction throughout, and my brother, Brian, for his help with the writing of several sections of this book.

The orchestra did *Scheherazade*, the *Pathétique*, and mine was Beethoven's Number One in C. It was a tremendous concert, one of those occasions when it is full and thrilling. It was the first time I had felt like that for a long time. In the early days I always experienced an onrush of emotion, because of newness and nervousness, and knowing how much the audience wanted from me – even ordered from me. But with professionalism some of that goes, worn off by the cunning and the craft that the soloist gathers and needs. You regulate yourself, pace yourself, use yourself and the orchestra to every good and mean advantage. But you lose that first pointed realization, the initial joy, and only rarely does it touch you again.

— from *Come to the War* by Leslie Thomas, with acknowledgments to the publishers Michael Joseph.

1

Beginnings

The first memories I have of cricket are of when we lived in Harbour Terrace, near Logan Park in Dunedin. The Water of Leith, a small stream which runs through some of the northern suburbs of the city, was only a few hundred yards away, and my brother and I, when we weren't playing cricket or rugby or hockey or tennis in the park nearby, spent many hours fishing in it for trout. Or if we weren't after the trout, if the stream was in spate, we'd be down at the boat harbour or the wharves fishing for butterfish and trevalli.

Our family shared an old wooden two storied house with my grandparents on my father's side. My grandfather, Louis, was a soccer fanatic having lived in Birmingham and played for West Bromwich Albion before emigrating to New Zealand when he was about twenty-one years old. The grandparents occupied the downstairs section of the house along with two cousins, Alan and Jimmy Larkins, who boarded with them. We, and a boarder, Alby Collins, lived upstairs. Alby was very keen on classical music and opera and he would retire to his room quite early some nights and play records for several hours. It was he who first awakened my interest in good music. Whenever he put Meyerbeer's *Les Patineurs* ballet suite on – I rather suspect he played it for our benefit more than his own – my elder brother, Brian, and I would shout out from our room which was diagonally across the hall, 'Turn it up, turn it up!' It was the lively nature of the piece that appealed to us at that age. I prefer Beethoven to Meyerbeer, but it was a start.

I was born on 26 May 1947 and was about eight or nine years old when we started to play 'serious' cricket on the concrete square in the back yard. We played diagonally across the square to pinch all the length we could out of the 'pitch' which couldn't have been more than fourteen yards long. Everyone joined in: my father, Brian, Alan, Jimmy, and sometimes Alby if he wasn't out playing tennis. As families go we were very sporting I suppose: my father had been an inter-provincial sprint cycling title-holder, and my brother, who was a much better-than-average cricketer, eventually played a few games of hockey for New Zealand and might well have played more if he hadn't become disenchanted. Alan had been a fine secondary-schoolboy athlete, won numerous national cycling titles, and was a member of the New Zealand Track Cycling team at the Melbourne Olympic Games in 1956.

Competition, then, was exceptionally keen. The men would tease Brian and me, haggling with us and disputing whether they were out or not, simply because we took it so seriously. This attitude on the part of the men made it all the more difficult for me to get the better of Brian. This was the big challenge, at least to equal him in performance, and never to admit to being inferior to him in any way. Three years makes a big difference at that age, and while I would accept, reluctantly, a beating, I never liked it and I gave absolutely everything I had in an effort to avoid it.

There was a long, narrow alley-way between our house and the one next door. The gap was wide of mid-on. If you could guide the ball down the alley you could just about run four before the fieldsman was able to get to it and return. If you hit the ball elsewhere in the yard there was only time to run a single. But down the alley was different. The fieldsman couldn't return the ball to the wicket from down there, he had to run all the way back to the yard with the ball before he could get the necessary arm-room to throw it back. If Brian or I chased it there'd be only three runs in it; with any of the others you might make four.

I made a point of trying to hit the ball down that alley as often as I could and I think this is one of the main reasons why, earlier in my career, I was stronger through mid-on, or certainly through the on side, than I was on the off.

16

If we weren't playing back-yard cricket we'd be out on the footpath with the ashcan or a butter box as a wicket. We played a lot of this sort of cricket a few years later when we were living in South Dunedin. Brian would come home from net practice with the first eleven and outside we'd go until dark. If I won the toss I'd bat all night if I could, until it became so dark we'd have to stop; and then the next night I'd insist on starting where I'd left off. We played with a tennis ball on a pitch of about sixteen or seventeen yards. The tennis ball would swing a bit, but with mostly only the two of us playing, the bowler having to field his own bowling, and lbw's almost impossible to agree on, it was difficult to get someone out. If you could drive the ball back past the bowler so that it missed all the parked cars and ran almost to the end of the block, then this was really rubbing it in to the poor bowler who had to retrieve it himself. Brian would sometimes throw his wicket away if he wanted a bowl. I never would; I knew I'd get a bowl sometime; I wanted to bat. I've got to the stage now where I could do with some of that adhesive fixation back again.

On the weekends we would play cricket ourselves or watch the seniors play and knock a ball about on the fringes of the Oval, Tonga Park, or Logan Park; all the usual places where Dunedin youngsters play. I was shorter than most boys of my age, so I played with a fierce determination at least to equal the performances of the best of the boys in my grade. The fact that I spent a few years in a class of kids whose ages ranged from five- to twelve- and thirteen-year-olds meant that I was continually playing against boys older than myself. I must have been a bloody irritation to some of the older kids, not only at cricket, but at rugby and hockey as well. Before I reluctantly gave up hockey I had played for the Otago representative side and, as a seventeen-year-old, had been a reserve for the South Island men's team.

When I went to Otago Boys' High School I became more serious about my cricket. The facilities there were rather better than I was accustomed to. Up till then I had always practised on artificial surfaces or in the back yard, but at OBHS there were proper grass practice strips, and with plenty of net practice I developed quickly and played for the school from 1962 to '64. It's true that I spent so much time playing sport that I neglected my studies. I remember one of the masters saying to me, 'Turner, I think it's about time you spent less time on sport and more on your school work. After all, you can't make a living playing cricket or any other sport in this country.' At that time there was much truth in what he said: neither of us could see into the future. I took little notice of his words, and almost every night after school, from about 3.30 p.m. to 5.30 p.m., there was nothing but cricket, or in the winter, hockey. I lived for sport, and enjoyed it far more than my studies.

It was while I was still at school that John Heslop, well known as a surgeon and enthusiastic cricketer, saw me playing in a second-grade club match on Littlebourne, the school ground. John was then an Otago selector. Apparently he was sufficiently impressed to ask me to travel to Invercargill to play for Otago in a trial match against Southland. I was lucky that day; things went my way. I went in at number five and was left not out 105. From there I was selected for the Otago Plunket Shield side at the age of seventeen. Looking back I have no regrets at having been put into first-class cricket so early, for I have always preferred to be tossed straight into the firing line and not to have to wait around.

Although I had seen some of our better players such as Sutcliffe, Dowling and Reid play, I never consciously set out to model my play on anything I'd seen them do. I knew they were good players, and in Bert Sutcliffe's case he was an extraordinarily fine player, but at that age I wasn't nearly acute enough to be able to analyse their batting, to identify their faults and strengths, and to learn from them. Besides, I was never one for hero worship – I suppose you could say I was far too involved in my own play. I was much more concerned with becoming a good player myself than in emulating or modelling my style and technique on that of other players. What helps a young player as much as anything in the early stages is the atmosphere surrounding the game at first-class

18

level when it is played as it should be played, seriously and hard, but with dignity and discipline. Inevitably you will be playing with noted players and as long as this doesn't overawe you it is a good influence and helps accelerate development.

I firmly believe that there is a right way and a wrong way of conducting oneself on the cricket field, and that regular displays of temper and tantrums are inexcusable. The occasional spontaneous outburst of temper is to be expected and can be allowed to pass, but I see no reason to make excuses for or condone the player who is prone to fits of pique and to hurl abusive language at his opponents. Officialdom is not obliged to make concessions to accommodate this sort of behaviour from players in any class of cricket.

It is not enough to say that anything goes on the cricket field, that what happens there should remain there. This attitude is little more than an attempted cover-up for immature behaviour. I see some logic in the point of view which says that an individual's true character, due to the pressures and stresses placed upon him during a tense cricket match, is often revealed by his actions in the course of a game.

I hold no brief either for those who use abuse as part of their repertoire of 'gamesmanship' – in fact gamesmanship doesn't really appeal to me at all. I think that it is a naive attitude to expect to be buddies over a beer off the field if you've spent a fair amount of time on it needling your opposition. I wonder how those who say anything goes on the field would react if the recipient of some particularly foul abuse, unable to contain himself, clouted the offender over the head with his bat. The point is that some instances, in cricket as in other games, warrant the taking of disciplinary action and the umpires are the people to see that it happens irrespective of the standing of a player.

I remember my first-class debut in 1964 very well. Otago were playing Canterbury at the Carisbrook ground in Dunedin. I was down to go in at number six and I remember sitting there in the players' enclosure, very much on edge, naturally, and wondering just how I'd measure up.

Otago had some good players at the time. Our captain, Jack

19

Alabaster, was one of the finest leg spinners in the world, and there were few finer opening seam bowlers anywhere than Frank Cameron. With these two as well as Jack's brother, Gren, in the side we had a very useful and varied attack. Although we had batsmen of the ability of Noel McGregor and Billy Ibadulla, our batting was usually brittle and not in the same class as our bowling.

Canterbury also had a good side that was chock full of 'name' players – Graham Dowling, Brian Hastings, Keith Thomson, Barry Hadlee, Dick Motz, Brian Andrews and John Ward. We batted poorly and it was therefore hardly surprising that Canterbury beat us comfortably by six wickets.

The day was sunny and very hot, conditions not all that common at Carisbrook, unfortunately. When our score was 80, that lovely stroke player Noel 'Snicker' McGregor was bowled by Dick Motz, one of New Zealand's finest-ever opening bowlers, who at that time was as quick as any bowler in the country. I remember being terribly keyed-up as I walked through the gate and out on to the park, feeling full of resolve without having the know-how to convert that resolve into results, all the while being extraordinarily conscious of the crowd around me and of the hot, sunny day. I was particularly worried about Dick Motz who appeared large and portly and full of menace. It was probably an injustice to have thought him portly at that stage of his career, for it was not until later on that he began to put on the beef. He always carried a bit 'extra' round his midriff, though, and this probably assisted his style of bowling.

I got off the mark first or second ball. I was a little late in coming down on it, nicking it wide of second slip. It was of catchable height but there was no third slip. The ball went down to the vacant third-man position but the Carisbrook outfield was so slow it didn't go for four. Everyone cheered very loudly and I think it was described later on as a late cut. I would settle for that; but it really was a nick just wide of slip in the air.

I stayed for nearly an hour getting to 10 before being given out lbw to the wily left-armer, Jack Kiddey. Some of the crowd disagreed with the decision and made their feelings known to the umpire. There was a bit of the old sympathy vote in their reaction. A couple of seasons later some of these very same supporters would have cheered the decision. Perhaps some of my more ardent critics will concede that at 10 runs an hour I made a racing start.

Even after this comparatively short innings I felt quite tired. I thought, how on earth can people stay out there and get hundreds? They must become absolutely exhausted. Anything like that seemed completely beyond me at that point.

I blocked my way through the rest of the season. At that stage an apt name for me would have been Glenn 'Block' Turner! In that first Plunket Shield season I scored the princely sum of 126 runs at an average of 14 per innings: I certainly occupied the crease for long enough to have scored a great many more than I did. Any records I set then would only have been for the fewest number of runs in the longest period of time.

Otago were playing a game against Central Districts at Cooks Gardens in Wanganui and I scored only 3 runs in the morning session. Then first ball after lunch I hit straight back past Vic Pollard for four – along the ground, of course, and so more than doubled my score. Gren Alabaster and I put on 136, Gren ending with 108 and I with 21 in 235 minutes. Obviously my innings must have been a proper yawn to watch but as far as the side was concerned it was very useful and not nearly as bad as it must have looked.

The ground at Cooks Gardens is encircled by a cycling track and Gren kept lobbing the ball on to it. The boundaries square of the wicket are very short and Gren had this uncanny knack of landing the ball just over the edge of the boundary where it kept bouncing on the track.

In the following two seasons, before I went to England, I started to play a little better, though always on the slow side. It was at this point that I started to feel the heat of criticism and to realise how mentally troublesome it can be. Some people, one or two journalists in particular, became so obsessed with my reputation for slowness that they seemed incapable of detecting any other qualities I might have shown as a player.

21

Any praise was grudgingly given: the mud that was then beginning to stick was, I sensed, going to be hard to remove.

My second first-class season, 1965–66 saw me finish second in the New Zealand first-class averages with 330 runs at 47.14, and this helped me gain selection for the President's XI against the touring M.C.C. side. I'd been going in at number three for Otago, but was asked to bat at number six in the game at Wellington. This didn't do much for my confidence because I've always preferred to be thrown in at the deep end at the start of an innings, rather than be nursed along lower in the order. I batted poorly, padding up to Peter Parfitt to be lbw for 5.

The game had some consolation for I had the pleasure of watching that extremely fine player, Colin Cowdrey, in action. Cowdrey had a magic of his own, seeming not only to have so much time to play the ball, but the attributes of poise and superb timing as well. Basil D'Oliveira said to me once, 'It is so damned annoying to field when Colin is batting, for although he only appears to push the ball past you it invariably just beats you to the boundary.'

During these first three years I came in for a lot of criticism from the crowds and from many players. Much of this criticism was justified, although those who thought I was getting pleasure out of not scoring as fast as they would have liked were mistaken. Quite simply I was learning and mostly refusing to throw my wicket away. To ask this of young players is to do them a disservice. Likewise the young player that bows to this pressure is revealing an understandable but regrettable weakness.

I have vivid memories of one match in particular. The opposition became visibly annoyed and agitated at the way I was blocking them out, so a couple of their fieldsmen literally began to throw the ball at me. Every time I pushed the ball at them I had to prepare to duck because I knew the ball was going to be rifled in, ostensibly aimed over the stumps, but really at me.

It was not surprising that at this time I was getting an ample share of criticism from the Press, perhaps more than my share. In time one learns to live with criticism, to realise that with some people first impressions will never be revised, that there will always be those who are consistently 'anti', just as there are those who are consistently 'pro'. The hardest criticism of all for any sportsman to take is that from journalists or anyone else who reveal themselves by the nature of their remarks as being unqualified to judge the players. Quite honestly I at times resented the way some journalists went about it, and I had to fight to dispel the impression that one or two were as interested in demolishing me as they were in my play.

There's not much a sportsman can do about newspaper criticism. By and large it's not the 'done thing', as it is in politics, say, to challenge one's critics. There are plenty of writers about who are sufficiently interested in a player to write about him often, yet whose interest has rarely, and in many cases never, extended to making the opportunity to discuss various aspects of the game with him. This is unfortunate because sports writers play such an important role in moulding the public's opinion of a game or a player. In my case I believe some people were so obsessed with the memory of what I *had been* that they were incapable of seeing me as I became. If I could make a plea, it is that the pundits concentrate their criticism on established players – without prematurely consigning them to the grave – rather than on young players just beginning to find their feet in a game.

One writer, in particular, who has often been critical of my cricket – as much through a misinterpretation of my cricketing philosophy and a thinly-veiled hostility towards English cricket and cricketers as anything else – felt impelled to write on a personal level, referring to my lack of physique and boyish appearance. To those who had not seen me play or listened to commentators describe my appearance this may have been interesting. In his report on the game between the President's XI and the M.C.C. he said I looked like a fourth-form school-boy coming to the wicket. That season I had scored more runs, I think, than any such schoolboy would have been capable of making in first-class cricket. The kindest thing that can be said about his remark is that it was thoughtless. Put it down to the so-called hyper-sensitivity of youth if you like, but at

23

that stage I was very sensitive about that sort of thing and felt hurt and upset. I mention this here, not because I hold any grudges against this writer now, but in the hope that others will spare future young players similar discomfort.

Early criticism, then, had the effect of forming a hard skin on me which was to be of great benefit later on, but its immediate effect was to inhibit me and this cost both myself and the spectators some cricketing enjoyment.

One of the vital aspects of cricket, or of any game I suppose, is not to allow yourself to become too emotional or affected by crowd behaviour. If you do become too emotional then you are likely to lose control and start playing rashly. I think you should at all times work out exactly what you are doing, and why, and then work assiduously to block out all the distractions possible.

When I look back on those first three years I feel it was valuable to have concentrated on defensive techniques. It seemed the natural way for me: there was no plot involved; it was not that I had decided that this was the way to begin a career, and that I would work on the attacking side of batting later. Basic to my nature was this very strong will to succeed, and while I was aware initially that I wasn't giving others or myself much enjoyment by occupying the crease for so long, I was scoring runs and this enabled me to hold my place in teams.

I received some invaluable coaching assistance at this stage. Although some very good players have been successful without ever having received much coaching, I think a good coach can be of tremendous assistance. By a good coach, I mean one who works on your natural ability and builds on it, not someone who wants you to play exactly the way *he played*. That sort of coach is usually critical of players who do not play the way he played: it is a kind of self-justification.

The game of cricket offers a lot more scope for individuality than many realise, and this should not be squashed. I do believe, though, that in the art of batting in particular, rather than bowling, there are one or two definite techniques that you must

24

endeavour to get right. The rest can then be left to the individual to bring in whatever flair he possesses.

The first coach I ever had was Lankford Smith, one of the best all-round cricketers in Otago's history. He contributed a great deal, not only by teaching me the basic strokes of batting, but also because of the encouragement I gained from having someone of his ability and experience as a player take an interest in me. Lankford was a *name!* a terribly important thing to a young player. I used to practise those techniques in front of a mirror. There were a dozen or so main strokes and I practised and practised them.

In my first couple of years in secondary school I was fortunate to be able to attend Bert Sutcliffe's coaching groups. Bert is recognised as one of the finest left-handers to have played the game. Here again, the mere fact that I was going to a coaching group run by someone of Bert's reputation was in itself of great value.

Later on Billy Ibadulla, the Warwickshire professional, came out from England as coach to the Otago Cricket Association for three years. In those three years he probably spent more time with me than any other individual – the only thing our family was able to do for him was to pass on a passion for trout fishing. Billy's first year in Otago coincided with my last at secondary school, and what he was able to provide was a rather more advanced stage of coaching than I'd had before at a time when I was ready to receive it. He used to get me down to Logan Park in the mornings before work at about 6.30 a.m. Others could have come if they'd been keen enough – they didn't seem to be, so Billy would just bowl and bowl and bowl to me. It was he who introduced me to county cricket: I certainly owe him a lot.

What Billy was ideally equipped to do was introduce me to the side of cricket other than the basic skills, to the psychological side if you like. I was able to listen to someone who could speak of famous players first-hand: of their techniques, attitudes, temperaments; of instances where various theories had been applied in practice in varying conditions and

25

circumstances, and of what the results had been. Billy had faith in my ability and, in a way, acted as a buffer against criticism at a time when I was most vulnerable to it. In so doing he was often stupidly and unfairly held responsible for my stodgy approach. I wish to debunk strongly this allegation which arose, as much as anything else, from a belief that English county cricket was defensive-minded, and that Billy was a disciple of it. Billy had been playing professional cricket for sixteen years so it didn't require much common sense or generosity to concede that he must have a fairly comprehensive knowledge of the game, so I decided to take notice of what he said and listen to his advice. I found it difficult to understand why a percentage of the local players did not. I should hate to think that my countrymen's main interest in visiting sportsmen from overseas was to see how often they could prove themselves superior to them, rather than to see how much they might learn from them.

Billy was not defensively-minded as a cricketer, and nor did I find county cricket so. If anything it is New Zealand cricket that is defensively-minded, but we can perhaps touch on that later. Whenever I was feeling a trifle depressed with the way things were going all Billy would say was this, 'Don't worry, Glenn, it will come, they will eat their words.' Consoling and encouraging.

Billy also taught me the importance of keeping my head *still* as opposed to *down*. So many coaches say, 'Keep your head down', when what they really mean is simply 'Watch the ball'. Your eyes should follow the ball, and your head move as little as possible. If you exaggeratedly go down over the ball, your head moves too much and you tend to overbalance. He also emphasised the importance of always being aware of where one's stumps were, and corrected a slight crouch that I had developed. This often happens in young players, and Billy got me to stand up more and use all the height I had, particularly when playing back for I tended to bend my right leg too much. This is a very common fault in a wide variety of players.

It was at this point that I had to think about what I was going to do when I left school. I was only an average pupil academically and I'd have had to struggle to get to University. I was enormously interested in sport and hardly at all in the scholastic side of school life. When I did leave school after having passed School Certificate I started work in an insurance office, and there I stayed for about thirteen months. I soon realised that this wasn't what I wanted to do. Then Billy came to me and said, 'I think you could do well in English county cricket, would you like to have a go?' At that stage I had never read a thing about county cricket: I knew nothing about it. My first reaction was to think that surely I wouldn't be good enough, but Billy said, 'Let me be the judge of that.' He then gave me an outline of the disadvantages and advantages of the life. I thought hard about it, for although it meant taking a risk, the idea appealed to me and gradually grew into something I really wanted to do. So I spent the next year or so working at Laurenson's, a Dunedin bakery. I worked on the night shift, taking bread off conveyor belts, crating it, and stacking the crates in bays. In this way I saved enough money to pay my fare to England.

I'd always believed – this is one aspect of youthful idealism that's encouraged – that a person should try to make a living out of something he really enjoyed doing. There were many who thought my decision was unwise, but I felt that even if I didn't make the grade I would at least have had a trip around the world. I planned to stop on the way and see as much as I could. There seemed to be nothing to lose.

It didn't take me long to find out that playing cricket professionally is hard work. There's nothing glamorous about it. It quickly becomes a job and has to be approached in that way. I tended to come back to New Zealand wanting more than anything else to relax, to do nothing more than simply walk along a deserted beach. While it was nice to make a few runs at home now and then I found it hard to work up the enthusiasm to go out and produce my best throughout the New Zealand season as well as the English one. I always felt as if I was on trial when playing at home, that other players were measuring their ability against me, that any runs I made in England meant very little to some people, and would continue to do

27

so, unless I produced similar performances at home in New Zealand.

Although I always liked, and still do, to play well in front of the home crowd, I often felt a trifle 'flat' after the strain of a full English season and this factor more than any other sometimes made it hard for me to lift my game at home in New Zealand.

2

A Contract with Worcestershire

Billy Ibadulla had arranged trials for me with Warwickshire, but just as I was about to leave New Zealand I received a letter from the captain Mike Smith saying that one of their committee members had almost certainly signed another over-seas player. However, he said by all means come as War-wickshire would honour their two-month contract even though they already had their full quota of overseas players. Billy had already left for England, via Pakistan, so I was unable to call on his advice. I was in a dilemma. I didn't understand the way things were organised in England. Should I go or shouldn't I? Finally I did decide to go and when I got there Mike Smith could not have been more helpful, even going to the lengths of bowling to me in the indoor nets and generally helping me in every way possible. Warwickshire gave me money for my kit and arranged for trials with other counties. They thought this was the wisest and fairest thing they could do.

By this time Billy had arrived back in England and I was able to ask him what he thought of the situation. Trials had been arranged with Worcester, Lancashire, Middlesex and Surrey. Worcester being only thirty miles down the road from Birmingham I decided to try there first.

The procedure was that I would have two days of nets which meant a morning and afternoon session on each day. The wickets were wet and favoured spin bowling, with the odd ball taking off a bit and pushing up a piece. Norman Gifford, Bob Carter and Doug Slade bowled to me in the nets. No one had to tell me to defend; this was my game anyway at that stage, but the conditions gave me good reason to. I don't think I hit one ball outside the net in the two days.

Deputed to watch me were Tom Graveney and Don Kenyon, and at the end of the two days it was decided to offer me a contract which was rather better than I had expected. Worcester offered me £650, which to me seemed quite good money for five and a half months, especially as an apprentice. I accepted the offer and did not take up the option of trials with other counties.

Those familiar with Worcester will know what a picturesque ground New Road is. There are delightful trees round the ground, the river Severn flows close by and in the background stands Worcester Cathedral. When I arrived in Worcester it was easily the most beautiful cricket ground I had seen. I still think there is none better.

For the first month I stayed with Billy and his family in Birmingham, travelling down the motorway by bus to Worcester. The logical thing to do was to shift down to Worcester and get a bedsitter. I did this and lived in this fashion for the first year. I went into digs for the next season, staying with Mrs. Rose Burnett and her husband, Jock. They looked after me like a son and cooked me hearty meals.

In my first season I played at least one second-eleven county match a week as well as a one-day club and ground match. Then on the weekends I played in the Birmingham league, as did all the second-eleven players. I played on Saturdays for Stourbridge in games which sometimes went on until eight in the evening. I did reasonably well in second-eleven cricket and spent the winter in Worcester in order to meet the one-year residential qualification required of overseas players at that time. That winter of 1967–68 is the only one I've spent in England.

During the winter the county arranged a job for me as a cardex clerk, which kept my bank balance level but no more, until I began the 1968 season as a member of the first team. In the early stages of the season I batted at number seven, sometimes at number six. At this time there were twenty-eight games in the County Championship and after playing fourteen games I had made only 418 runs at the rather poor average of 17. Then, without warning, I was given a go at opening the innings. In my remaining ten games of the season I scored

764 runs at an average of 42. I managed to total 1,182 at an average of 29 for the complete season which wasn't too bad for a new comer to English cricket.

I didn't realise it then, but I had got Duncan Fearnley, the other opener, the sack. Subsequently I became closely associated with Duncan as he made bats with my autograph on them. Nowadays he feels that I did him a great favour, although in those days he was very jealous of me. He is certainly making more money out of his business activities than he did out of playing cricket.

Duncan had seven years on the Worcester staff without being capped, mainly because he played during some of Worcester's good years. Worcestershire were one of the most successful county sides in the sixties winning the County Championship twice, in 1964 and 1965, and finishing runners-up in 1962 and 1966. They were also in two Gillette Cup finals. Worcester had a fairly stable side over this period, so the only opportunities to play first-team cricket that came Duncan's way were when someone else was injured. It was hardly going to matter how well he did for as soon as the other chap was fit Duncan was going to be out of the side again. I think Duncan would probably have done better in another county side. He was certainly good enough to have played a lot more first-team cricket than he played with Worcestershire.

When I started opening my performance improved considerably, and so did my attitude towards things in general. I had been so cautious and reserved that I had been going to bed at about nine o'clock at night, not drinking at all, trying to do everything possible that was right. I found that even though I was going to bed early I wasn't getting a satisfactory sleep. In fact, what happened was I tossed and turned until midnight, worrying about what I was going to do the next day. Finally I said to myself, 'to hell with it!' I wanted to get more enjoyment out of my cricket, to relax more, and this new attitude, I think, started to come out in my cricket. I began to play so much better. While it was true I started to keep later nights, I tried to be sensible about it and get a fair amount of sleep.

When it came to alcohol I tried a very unscientific trial and error basis, and sometimes suffered as a result. Eventually, and many sore heads later, I found that if I had my few gin and tonics and went to bed around eleven, I was able to get eight or nine hours' sound sleep and I felt more relaxed all round. When you're playing cricket virtually seven days a week, for week after week, it's essential to try and live normally otherwise you'd go 'around the bend', as we say in New Zealand or, as they say in England, 'around the twist'.

Glenn Turner: a 1974 portrait

Four former captains of Otago Boys' High School first XI photographed when Otago played Central Districts at Wanganui in 1965. They are Glenn Turner (1964), Des McCawe (1931), Alec Priest (1926) and Frank Hutchison (1913)

Turner is given out lbw to Peter Parfitt in the match between the M.C.C. and the President's XI at Wellington in 1966

3

Playing for New Zealand

I was first selected to play for New Zealand in 1969. It was for a home series against the West Indies who stopped over in New Zealand on the way home from their tour of Australia. I was just twenty-one at the time and I think many people thought it was a bit early for me to be selected for New Zealand. They felt I was a little too young to be opening a test innings and that I'd hardly played enough first-class cricket to have acquired the necessary background and reputation. ·I didn't feel that I was too young or that I'd had insufficient experience. I had, after all, played three seasons in New Zealand as well as two in England and this added up to a total of about fifty first-class games. I suppose many people hadn't seen all that much of me and that others thought I was being selected as a result of my English experience and were sceptical of the value of this. Anyway, I made the classic inauspicious start to a test career by getting out for a duck at Eden Park, caught Sobers bowled Hall. At least I chose to fall to a couple of good ones.

Before the series against the West Indies I'd had a reasonably successful Plunket Shield season including scores of 167 against Wellington, an innings that took an awfully long time and which irritated and frustrated the Wellington players immensely, and 77 against Auckland. By the end of the test series I had totalled 708 runs for the season ('68–'69) from 17 innings which gave me the respectable average of 47.20.

In a summary of the Plunket Shield season, R.T. Brittenden wrote of my 'distinctly professional batting'. I suppose this was a nice way of saying that I didn't give anything away and that I looked as if I knew what I was about. He also wrote that I 'certainly (looked) good enough to be given a test trial'. Every-

33

one in New Zealand was noticeably wary of me at this stage of my career, for at that point it wasn't known if I would be available for the coming tour of England or not, but I always felt that Brittenden was one of those on my 'side', if only just.

The highlight of the first test played in Auckland, and which the West Indies won by five wickets, was Bruce Taylor's 124. His century was scored in the startlingly short time of 86 minutes. Having made a duck in the first innings and 40 in the second innings of my first test match I felt about as insignificant and out of place as it was possible to feel – Brittenden wrote that I was 'pale and tense, without a hint of (my) usual engaging grin' – but my main reaction to Taylor's innings was a mixture of astonishment, mirth and admiration at such a brazen display. Only an innocent, a laconic disrespecter of reputations could have played an innings such as Taylor played that day.

The West Indians won largely through the efforts of Seymour Nurse who scored 168 in the second innings to add to his earlier 95. Nurse, though playing well, had fortune on his side in a match that could have gone either way.

The second test at Wellington was a memorable one for us. We batted last and won by six wickets. Here I was enjoying a test victory in only my second test for New Zealand – dozens of cricketers before me had played for New Zealand for many years and never tasted victory in a test match.

The Basin Reserve was kind to me, as it often has been since, and I got to 74 before Sobers made an athletic spring to his right at short mid-on and took a good catch to dismiss me off Edwards. I'd thought the ball was on the way for four, but I was philosophical about it as Sobers had put me down in the slips when I was only 12. With this innings I felt I had gone a good way towards convincing people that I was worthy of a place in the New Zealand test side and that, perhaps, I had cemented my place for the series. I'd even hit a few balls to the boundary which may have surprised and, I hope, pleased some of my critics.

Bryan Yuile, Brian Hastings and Ross Morgan eventually saw us to victory, but it was the hostile, splendid pace bowling of Dick Motz, especially in the West Indies' first innings when he took 6 for 69, that lingers longest in my mind. That, and the satisfaction of winning.

Then it was on to Christchurch for the third test where Seymour Nurse made 258 and Joey Carew 91 out of the West Indies' first innings total of 417. Dick Motz, with but one wicket under his belt and the West Indies 326 for 2, came back at them and in the space of 27 balls took another four wickets for seven runs to finish with the fine figures of 5 for 113.

When we went in I was first out for 30 when the total was 53. I played Lance Gibbs down into the pitch and the ball spun back and hit my stumps. In panic and despair, sensing the danger, I searched for the ball but couldn't find it. Everyone else on the ground seemed to know where it was except me. Afterwards my cousin Tom Eggleton joked with me about it, saying that I was 'digging around looking for it like a bloody ant'.

It was a matter of some pride for us that after following on 200 behind we battled it out to reach 367 for 6 and saved the match. Again it was the ubiquitous Brian Hastings who played the vital hand in what was a good team effort, by being there 117 not out at the close. I scored 38 runs myself.

During this tour, Wes Hall and Charlie Griffith were by this time past their best. Griffith only bowled really quickly at the Basin Reserve, but he didn't get any more out of the wicket than Ross Edwards who, off a short run, got as much out of the pitch as anyone. The West Indian Board of Control actually announced their team to tour England while the second test was in progress and this caused a degree of embarrassment and unhappiness amongst the West Indian side, especially among those players who were left out. Edwards was one, and I'm sure this was a mistake as he was just the type of bowler who would have done well in England. The decision to announce the team at that point was at best thoughtless, at worst heartless.

At that time the attitude of the New Zealand team to tests was somewhat negative. Our attitude seemed more 'not to lose' than 'out to win'. We had little confidence in our ability. Nowadays we do feel we have a chance in each match although

35

we have not always played with as much initiative as we might have.

In 1969 New Zealand went on a short tour of the United Kingdom, after the West Indies had toured. Worcester released me for the second half of the English season and I joined the New Zealand team at Bradford for the game against Yorkshire. I recall a lot of the boys getting out before the match and lapping the park and sprinting about. Because I'd already played concentrated cricket for half a season I'd go out and have a knock up and a few catches instead. I wasn't prepared to become a marathon runner or anything like that. It must have looked to some that I wasn't fitting in and Graham Dowling surprised me by pointing out that I wasn't with Worcester any longer, I was with New Zealand, and I ought to show a bit more enthusiasm. Perhaps he was unaware of how hard a county player has to work: I wasn't prepared to concede that I needed to get myself fired up at all, I was well in gear already.

Bruce Murray played consistently well throughout the tour. His driving was good and the other very good aspect of Bag's play was his temperament – it took an awful lot to upset him. Brian Hastings and Vic Pollard also came to light with some good innings during the tour.

It was on this tour that I began to field at first slip and by the end of the tour I had acquired the reputation of being very useful in this position. Some observers felt I stood too fine and said so; some have continued to say so. If I had been missing catches as a result of where I was standing I would have given this criticism a lot of thought, but as I wasn't it didn't concern me much. Even though I was standing finer than most slips do (and I still do), I found that I was still taking catches on my left off right-hand batsmen. The major factor which influenced my positioning in the first place was the methods employed by our wicketkeeper, Ken Wadsworth. I found that often, when a ball was bowled down the line of the off stump, Ken would move slightly to his left to take the ball. But if a batsman went after a half volley pitching fairly wide, Ken would tend to follow it and quite often ended up catching the ball in front of first slip. It is generally accepted that most snicks off the quick bowlers go fine, to the 'keeper or to first or second slip. The next most common area is gully. I believe that, particularly with the new ball which flies fairly quickly, if you can catch everything round about you then you're more than doing your job. There's nothing more frustrating for the opening bowlers than to have the ball flying between the slips and the 'keeper. If the slips are standing wide this is much more likely to happen.

To a slow bowler who's bowling over the wicket I stand with my left foot on the extension of the line of the return crease. If the ball is bowled slightly wide I anticipate the batsman's shot and start moving wide. If the ball is dropped short and the batsman's going for the cut, I stand up and move wide looking for the top edge. Now and then the batsman gets a bottom edge and this can make you look a bit silly, but I always go for the biggest percentage, which is the top edge. You have to stand up for these as they tend to grow big on you. I found my methods worked fairly well and resulted in my taking several catches off the slow bowlers by anticipating and moving wide. The best example of this was catching Geoff Boycott at Lord's. He virtually cut Vic Pollard off the middle of the bat and when I caught him by having anticipated the shot and moving wide he was astonished and very annoyed. I'm sure he felt, as he played the shot, that he'd played it well and was expecting runs from it, certainly not to lose his wicket.

Most first slips and a lot of second slips watch the ball right from the time it leaves the bowler's hand, though in the case of second slip some watch only the edge of the bat. Alan Ormrod, who stands alongside me at Worcester, is a very good slip and he watches the edge of the bat, so it is something of a personal thing.

I feel first slip is a very good position from which to captain a side. You know exactly how a batsman's playing and how your bowler is performing. You are able to work out angles for field placements and you are ideally positioned to view the play from the batsman's angle.

The weather for most of New Zealand's tour of England was magnificent, though in early May the Worcester ground was

37

under six foot of water. My most vivid memory of the tour is of the first test match at Lord's. This match remains prominent in my mind mainly because of the things that went wrong. The things that go wrong always tend to stick in my mind rather better than those times when I, or the side I've been playing for, have done well. I am always trying to remember the mistakes made in an attempt to avoid repeating them.

The first test at Lord's was all over twenty minutes before stumps on the second to last day. The weather forecast for the U.K. was bad – for mainly geographical reasons forecasts for the U.K. are usually more accurate than they are in New Zealand – and the rain that was already falling and moving across from the west was obviously soon to hit London. I knew that if we could see out the day then there was a very good chance that the final day would be washed out. It did rain, so if we'd managed to survive for another twenty minutes then the weather would have saved us.

I'm afraid we played very, very badly indeed that day. We played amateurishly and showed little fight. So many of our side just slogged out.

There is a school of thought that maintains that if you're in difficulties, or are in the middle of a bad 'trot', you might as well see if you can slog your way out of it. I disagree: the only way I can see of recapturing any sort of form is to play a long innings. On that day at Lord's, I remember Basil D'Oliveira coming to me after a wicket had fallen and saying, 'After a shot like that, that chap ought to be sent home on the next boat.' This was the way the English side felt. We'd have earned far more respect if we'd fought to save the match.

In this test we experienced all sorts of problems with Derek Underwood, particularly in the second innings, after a shower of rain had fallen on the wicket. This made him even more difficult and we were bowled out for 131. I batted throughout the innings in this match to remain 43 not out.

In some reports of the match it was suggested that I should have taken more off Underwood. I don't think Dick Motz, our opening bowler, had this complaint for he spent the night in hospital after being hit a nasty blow in the groin by the England paceman, Alan Ward. Dick's complaint was that I hadn't taken enough off Ward. He said he'd have been more than happy with Underwood. The truth was that the ball was moving about a good deal and I simply wasn't good enough to take the strike whenever I wanted. I'm afraid I found it as difficult to survive as anyone else.

Soon after that match I broke a knuckle in a match against Minor Counties, a game that was really of little importance to us. So for three weeks I had my forearm in plaster. The accident was unusual. I had been fielding in the slips throughout the tour where considerable concentration is required if you are to do the job properly. I asked Vic Pollard, the acting skipper for the match, if I could go out into the outfield where the pressure is off and have a bit of a run around. He said okay and I was put out to graze on the boundary edge. The ball was swept or 'lapped' towards me at deep backward square leg. I came forward to it as it looked as if it wasn't going to carry, but in the end I misjudged it slightly and had to stretch so far for it that I got it on the end of my finger. Instead of breaking a bone towards the tip of my finger I broke the knuckle on my left hand. This left me with absolutely no chance of playing in the second test at Trent Bridge. I was annoyed and disappointed as I knew, and subsequent experiences have borne this out only too well, that a player needs to be playing regularly in order to retain form and score consistently well.

The second test at Trent Bridge was remarkable only for the improved batting from our side and the lamentable bowling of our pace attack. The match was rain-affected and this was perhaps a good thing for us as England feasted royally on our bowlers' generous fare making 451 for 8 declared in reply to our 294. We were 66 for 1 when the rain eventually forced a conclusion to proceedings.

We were due to play Sussex in our last game before the third and final test at The Oval. I told our skipper, Graham Dowling, that I would like to try and play in the game against Sussex as the plaster had by then been taken off my hand. I was very keen to play in the third test, and I felt the Sussex match would give me an opportunity to see how fit I was. Dowling decided, though, that it would be better if I did not play in the Sussex match and had a few nets as preparation instead, for it was their intention irrespective to play me in the test.

To go into any test match with only a few nets behind you is not the ideal kind of preparation at any time. I found then, and I've noticed it often since, that to have had only net practices between tests is a bad thing. You tend to go out into the middle and play what almost amounts to a net innings. In other words you play much too freely. This is what happenned to me at The Oval. I played and missed a lot, although in other respects my form in scoring 53 was quite good. In fact, in many ways I played more freely than I'd played previously on the tour.

I thought a lot about this innings and nowadays, for a couple of nets before an important match, I tighten up and try to play the way I will have to play in the early stages of an innings. Eventually one, of course, wants to play freely in an innings, but I think it is vital, for an opening batsman, to play close to himself, particularly when the ball is new and the quick bowlers are fresh. This obviously helps eliminate errors.

In this final test Bevan Congdon and I were going along quite nicely and the score had reached 68 for 1 when a shower of rain, which was to change the whole complexion of our innings, drove us from the field. Shortly after we returned to the field Underwood came on, the ball popped and turned and we were all out for 150. I was given out caught at slip to a ball I felt I hadn't hit, something that concerned me more then than it does now.

Though we were able to dismiss England for a modest 242 our second innings score of 229 was not enough and England won by 8 wickets.

I feel we made a mistake on that tour by not asking for test-match covering of wickets in county matches. When we did get rain in two of the test matches, at Lord's and The Oval, things really did go against us. If we had had experience earlier in the tour of playing against county sides on wickets that were damp, we would have handled the conditions we experienced in the test matches much better. On New Zealand's recent 1973 tour of England we did ask for test-match covering of wickets and this helped improve our performance, whereas in 1969 we had full coverage of wickets.

Test-match covering of wickets is something very different from the method which operates for county matches. Once a county match is started the covers are removed and are left off, night and day, for the duration of the three days. Test-match covering means that once a ball has been bowled in a day's play, the covers are left off for the remainder of that day, or until play is abandoned for the day. I think we felt that if we had test-match covering only during the county matches in 1969, then we might lose some playing time. I don't think this would have happened because the bowler's approach and four feet of the wicket in front of the popping crease are always covered. This means that where the bowler's foot comes down and the area of the first pace of his follow-through are kept dry. As a result play is seldom lost, for the wicket itself rarely becomes saturated to the point where the ball splashes on landing, making a divot or spraying in the batsman's eye before the ball arrives.

It was sad that we performed so poorly in the U.K. because we went on to India and Pakistan immediately after the English tour and played so very well. We had left the English public with the impression that it was nice to have had these young men over from New Zealand; they do run around with great enthusiasm on the field, but they're not up to much else. They thought that we were still very much a poor relation as far as cricket was concerned and didn't really provide much of a contest for the English side. This was unfortunately true of the showing we put up in England in 1969.

4

On Tour in India, 1969

We left England for Bombay in mid-September determined to try to improve on our rather dismal performances against the English side. Naturally we were expecting fine weather so it was a surprise to hear our Boeing captain announce that it was raining in Bombay as the monsoons were going on for longer than usual. This rain was to interfere with our practices prior to our first match in India.

I shall never forget the drive of about fifteen miles from Santa Cruz airport, Bombay, into the city. Some of the things we saw were, for us, incredible. It was still quite early in the morning, and we passed hundreds of people lying asleep on the sides of the road. Many were stretched out on the pavement with not even a sack to lie on. We saw people openly relieving themselves on the side of the road. When you think of it, what else could they have done? All this came as quite a shock to us, for even though we'd read about this sort of thing, we literally had to see it to believe it.

Almost everyone who'd been on a tour of India before had warned us of the rigours involved. In spite of this, I was quite looking forward to it, educationally as much as anything, and if I did get ill I felt, rather perversely perhaps, that this too would be an experience. Quite honestly, I would far sooner tour a country like India than somewhere where the conditions and surroundings are more familiar.

Before we left England, Hugh Burry, the former All Black rugby footballer and now a doctor at Guy's Hospital in London, provided us with some drug in the form of pills which proved to be almost totally effective. We all knew what had happened to the New Zealand side in 1965, and we were alarmed at the thought of the same thing happening to us. The management were determined to do everything they could to get the side through with as little illness as possible.

There seemed to be no limit to the variety of illnesses one could get in India, so one member of the side – who shall remain anonymous – rather morbidly ran a sweepstake on who would get ill first. This scheme resulted in some hilarity. Each player had different odds placed on him; I think I was odds-on favourite to go down, partly because I've never, by any stretch of the imagination, looked like a tough guy, and partly because I have peculiar tastes when it comes to food. Frankly, though I'm no gourmet, I am very fussy about my food. I don't eat the best food money can buy, I don't eat fruit of any description, and I loathe jam, but what I do like, I like very much indeed. I'm very fond of curry, and I just love ice cream – in fact I started a lot of the Worcester boys off on ice cream and several now rank as connoisseurs. So it wasn't going to be easy to please me.

The surprising thing was that none of us was ill for a long time. Dick Motz had gone home from England with a back injury and when we eventually decided we needed a replacement David Trist was sent out from New Zealand. David, poor fellow, became ill almost immediately, but it had nothing to do with the food. It was a type of travel sickness. In the end no one won any money in the sweepstake, which was a good thing. We were all so conscious of the health side of things that at times our behaviour bordered on the absurd. Take the business of cleaning our teeth, for example. We were encouraged to clean them in soda water, Coke, or Fanta – anything but water. Water was taboo and none of us ever drank it. No one was able to convince me that water could do me much more harm than Coke, but I went along with the rule just the same. I took to Fanta as it is less fizzy than Coke and easier on the throat. Some of us found that we were drinking about twenty to thirty bottles a day. Even when it came to drinks on the field, Fanta was still the most popular. We also took care to ensure that the cold drinks were not ice cold or we'd have run the risk of suffering stomach cramps.

It wasn't always easy to apply the rules. If you asked for Fanta in the Indian clubs ice would invariably be put in it and we would have to refuse it. We quickly found out that it wasn't enough to send the waiters back with the same drink because they would just go behind the doors and pull the ice out with their fingers. So we asked them to leave the drink with us and would they please get us another one.

We had arranged for some New Zealand beer to be sent over. But as most of it didn't arrive we were rationed to only two cans per head per match. This hardly quenched our thirst so the non-drinkers in the side become very popular.

Indian liquor wasn't easy to come by either. Bombay in particular was a dry area at that time, and you needed a permit to drink there. We also found that the local beer, though tasting all right had a drastic, near-instantaneous effect. You didn't have to wait till the next morning for a headache. There was a headache in every bottle, and it wasn't until the latter stages of the tour, after talking to Indrajit Singh, who played the last test against us after Engineer had been injured, that we learnt the secret of how to get rid of the headache in the beer. He maintained you had first to get rid of the glycerine in the beer. Pataudi, though, did not believe there was glycerine in the beer. He reckoned it was far too expensive a commodity for them to put in. But Indrajit was adamant, so for the rest of the tour we would get the barman to open a bottle and quickly put the neck into a glass of cold water. One could immediately see a heavy liquid sinking to the bottom of the glass. After the reaction had ceased, we would drink what was left in the bottle. Normally only a very little of the quantity was lost. It may have been a psychological thing, but after that we found the beer reasonable and, more importantly, the headaches disappeared.

Brabourne Stadium in Bombay became our first place of residence. We couldn't have been closer to the cricket ground, but the beds were so hard that if you flopped on them without thinking there was a risk of breaking your back! Unfortunately my room had no air-conditioning, only a fan, and at first I found it very difficult to sleep at nights.

Most of us straightaway bought some jandals, called 'flip-flops' in the U.K. and 'chappals' in India. When we wore them, our feet proved to be of great fascination and amusement to the locals. It was the whiteness more than anything. There was much pointing and chuckling, and when some of the boys started wearing shorts it was cause for even more mirth. And when they saw us sun bathing! – well, they thought 'that's the end, they are trying to become like us and ours is built-in!'

There is a wild enthusiasm for cricket in India. A quite remarkable number of people come to watch the games. Whenever we met strangers we were always asked the same question. 'What is your name, saab? What is your name?' I felt that I could not ignore them, so I told them. Then all of a sudden it would go round the group like wildfire and there would be a low chant of, 'Turner, Turner, Turner, Turner,' or 'Murray, Murray, Murray, Murray,' or whatever the name was. Of course they speak in a very guttural way, which makes it sound so much more appealing and amusing. But I was asked the question so often that I eventually got tired of saying my name. I decided to start calling myself Mahatma Turner and see what happened. As soon as I said that they looked stunned and viewed me very strangely. Maybe it saved me from telling my name so often. Apparently 'mahatma' translated means 'the great spirit'. I hoped they wouldn't feel that I was insulting them by putting myself in the same category as, say, Mahatma Gandhi. Maybe they felt I had awesome aspirations.

We had a week to prepare for our first game at the Brabourne Stadium against the Indian Combined Universities side, but two of those days were rained off, and this interfered with our preparation. I remember only too well the first appearance we made at the stadium. Graham Dowling had us in training straightaway. I'm afraid after two circuits most of us were right out of breath. There was virtually no movement of air at all in the stadium; it was so still and the humidity was high. These two laps were just too much of a struggle. In fact, after we had completed these and gone through one or two physical exercises we hardly had any energy left for net practice so our

46

first day was mostly wasted time. Mark Burgess had played in an Invitation match in India the year before and I said to him, 'How on earth could you stay out in this heat and score a hundred?' which was exactly what he had done without having had the time to acclimatise. I have since become more used to hotter climates and can manage it now, but at that time I couldn't see how it was going to be possible to occupy the crease for too long. In all earnestness I said to the boys, 'Well, we'll have to try and get our runs a bit more quickly over here because we aren't going to be able to stay in the middle for too long.' The suggestion of me trying to get on with the job more quickly really amused them.

As the Australians were going to tour after us, we were not to play in any of the major centres apart from Bombay. By playing in Ahmedabad, Nagpur, Indore and Hyderabad we missed out on the major centres of Calcutta, Madras, Kanpur and Delhi.

It wasn't long before we met evidence of how emotional things can become in India. After playing the university match in Bombay we were due to go to Ahmedabad to play the first test match, but as a result of Muslim-Hindu rioting there it was thought it would be unwise for us to go. So we stayed in Bombay. The Nawab of Pataudi, a Muslim, said we would be a damn sight safer in Ahmedabad than he would, and he wasn't having any of the idea of going up there. Abid Ali was also anything but keen on the idea. This rescheduling left only a matter of four days to prepare a test strip. Hardly long enough.

Fortunately we travelled by plane in India: their trains have a poor reputation. Indian Airlines flies similar planes to some of those in New Zealand – Fokker Friendships. One aspect that irked us a little was that the two men assigned to us by the Cricket Club of India, and who were to help us so much throughout the tour, could not fly around with us. Quite often they had to leave a couple of days before us, go by train, and give themselves time to prepare things for our arrival. They were not provided with accommodation; they either slept in the hallway or in the dressing rooms if the facilities were better there. We were never really able to come to terms with this, and felt that the treatment meted out to these chaps was rather unfair. The test itself was a dismal effort by us. We lost by 60 runs, collapsing in the second innings to the spin of Bedi and Prasanna.

From Bombay we went on to Indore, where the facilities were, not surprisingly, nowhere near the equal of those in Bombay. The ground, on which quite a lot of hockey is played, was more than adequate, but the hotel was not. I shall never forget it. Conditions were fairly primitive, and the cockroaches were even more numerous than usual. The standard practice was to take off one's shoe and prepare to belt them. After dark it was even worse; if you switched the light on quickly you wouldn't know where to start. But we'd have a real go at them for all that, even though the Indian people didn't like us doing this. Their belief in the possibility of reincarnation in other than human form is very strong, and as far as the people were concerned we might have been killing their grandmother or some closer relative.

The hotel was a fair way from the ground so we were provided with an old bus to travel in. Our driver could not speak even one word of English. In fact we knew more Hindi than he knew English. We were able to greet him Indian style by saying 'namaste' and putting our hands together just below the level of our chin. He would return the greeting, exaggerating the same movement, and would say 'namaste' several times: 'Namaste, namaste, namaste, saab.' We learned that his name was something very close to Barrabas so after a while that's what we started calling him. The bus had a quaint big horn near the driver's seat, which Barrabas used to squeeze. The first thing you do, it seems, when you get into any vehicle in India, is to start blowing the horn. I don't know why they bother, but everybody does it, even though nobody seems to take much notice.

The roads in India are often covered with people and livestock and in Indore there were cows all over the place. Nobody seems to be in much of a hurry or concerned about the possibility of being knocked down.

48

Don Kenyon goes out to make his last appearance at New Road, with Turner as junior partner, in the match between Worcestershire and Pakistan in 1967

The first test at Lord's, 1969: Geoff Boycott is caught at slip by Turner off Victor Pollard's bowling

Hendricks watches as Gibbs is driven square to the boundary
in the Worcestershire vs West Indies match

About to catch Gavaskar in the match against Indian
Combined Universities at Bombay, 1969. When Hastings
knocked the ball up, "I nipped across and caught it behind
him at gully."

We were coming back from the ground one evening, and Barrabas wasn't wasting any time. Most of the team knew the Hindi word for hurry, which is *juldi*. Suddenly Vic Pollard yelled out from the back, '*Juldi, juldi*, Barrabas.' That was all it needed. Barrabas went berserk and put his foot down flat. The old bus took off and livestock and people were dashing out of the way in front of us. The horn was blowing continuously and it became dangerous, quite beyond the joking stage. Unfortunately nobody knew the word for slow down. It was after this incident that we made sure that we did add it to our very limited vocabulary. Everyone was shouting 'Slow down, you fool! Take it easy!' Barrabas did nothing of the kind. He thought that we were encouraging him. So he went faster and faster until, miraculously, we reached our hotel without accident. How he did it I will never know.

The second test was at Nagpur. A test had never been played there before. Nagpur is right in the centre of India, and we were told that it would be really hot there. Our accommodation was not what we'd expected. We stayed in small houses around a compound, houses similar to those used by the British before Indian independence. Each building could accommodate up to four players. Meals were eaten in a separate building. We had mosquito nets on our beds. I had never slept under one before and although it was a little hotter under it I was grateful for the protection it offered.

In Bombay each player had been presented with a torch which had inscribed on it, 'The first Test Match New Zealand v. India, 1969'. At that time we thought it was a strange sort of thing to give us. We didn't know then how useful they were to be in Nagpur. After the mosquito nets were tucked in around us, the first thing we did was to switch on the torch and kill any mosquitos that were inside the net.

When we were in England some of the English side had told us the story of how, on an earlier tour of India, a baboon had actually walked through their rooms. At that time I thought it sounded like a tall story. Now I can quite believe it because there were a number of baboons in the trees surrounding the compound. Some actually came down and walked

49

through the place from time to time. Although they seemed pretty harmless on an individual basis, I shouldn't like to rile a band of them as they could turn nasty. Vic Pollard wasn't worried by them and rather enjoyed chasing the odd one around the place.

When we went down to the ground to practise the day before the match, we were astounded by what we saw. The facilities were primitive. Temporary stands were erected which appeared to be little more than bamboo sticks tied with binder-twine. They were so makeshift and unstable that during the match different sections collapsed, making quite a commotion. Again we were astounded when we saw that the roller was being towed up and down the wicket by a water buffalo. The outfield was being cut in the traditional way by hand-mowers. Our changing room could have been Grand Central Station; every Tom, Dick and Harry kept walking through it. People peered in through the windows. There was certainly no privacy. We could hardly complain because the Indian team had even worse conditions. They had to change up on top and their dressing room had only a canopy for a roof and no walls. It was here that Faroukh Engineer chipped a bone in his foot when trying to get up the ladder which led to this makeshift dressing room.

We were already one down in the series and felt it was vital to win the toss. We did this and batted first but by lunch on the first day the pitch had become like a beach. It soon became a dust bowl and remained like this for the rest of the match. Our batting was hardly cavalier but we totalled 319 and 214 which was good enough to give us a win by 167 runs.

While in Nagpur we got to know an American who was in the Peace Corps and he was keen to show us the village where he was living and working. A group of us went with him and we were able to get a very good idea of exactly how eighty per cent or more of the Indian people live. What appeared to be a primitive little village, in reality housed over a thousand people. The American lived in a hut himself, very much as the villagers lived. The path into the village was narrow, like a deer trail, and the village comprised mud huts with thatched roofs. One of the women had a bucket containing a mixture of water and cow-manure which she was slapping on the side of one of the huts with her hands. You could say it acted as a form of plaster. Although she was shy at first she finally consented, after some persuasion from our American friend, to carry on so that one or two of our boys could take photos. Everything seemed authentic India. Women were coming to the well and carrying water away on their heads in large water vessels made of clay. Further on we came upon a potter working on his wheel, making water vessels. This fellow, who was completely bald, was very keen to show us his skill. He'd hardly begun when another Indian came along and pushed him out of the way. This was the head potter; the other was a mere learner. The head potter then proceeded to show us how it was done, while others sat around and gave him plenty of advice on the shaping of the vessel. His advice to them, which was translated for us by our friend, was that they should shut up and keep quiet as he was the one making the jug.

The American explained how difficult it was to get new ideas across to these people. Their methods were tried and tested over centuries, and they were frankly afraid to use new techniques and implements in their farming in case they failed. They had faith in what they knew. If they were to be misled then so many more would starve and die. In spite of all the starvation and hunger they were reluctant to try to eradicate the insects that were destroying their crops, as they didn't believe in interfering with the course of nature. The farmers were prepared to sit back and watch, not happily but philosophically perhaps, insects destroy half their crop. We left that village much chastened by the realisation that more than eighty per cent of nearly 600 million people lived in the manner of these villagers.

The third and final test match in India was played in Hyderabad and, like Nagpur, it was the first time a test had been played there. The Lal Bahadun Stadium was quite new with a capacity of about 35,000 people, in comparison to the

50,000 capacity of the Brabourne Stadium in Bombay. Once again we stayed at the stadium itself where the facilities were excellent.

We decided to announce our side the day before the match. We had watched the wicket being prepared and, as is common in India, they put some manure on it. This seems to fill in the cracks that develop in the pitch. We felt at that time that they were trying to produce a wicket that would turn because our side had mainly seamers. But in the end we were fairly satisfied that there was no foul play intended.

We were to experience more rioting in this game than ever before. We totalled an extremely modest 181, then the Indians started about as badly as it's possible to start, and were soon 49 for 9 wickets, but their last pair of Bedi and Venkataraghavan put on 40 more runs before Bedi's wicket fell about half an hour before stumps. One of the spectators was so elated at the performance of the last pair that he came out to pat them on the back. Up till this point no one had been allowed on the field and one of the older policemen ran out after him carrying a *danda*, a long bamboo stick which is used to quieten the mobs. Usually they hit people around the legs, never above the waist. The spectator was young and too fast for the old policeman, so he threw the *danda* at him. This whistled over the young chap's head landing a few yards in front of him. In the meantime more policemen had come on to the field to assist their colleague. As soon as the spectator saw this he attempted to pick up the bamboo stick to defend himself. Just as he bent down, one of the policemen took a swing and the stick hit him above the eye. There was blood everywhere and he went down yelling and screaming. That was the end of things because the crowd started rioting in sympathy. Rioting in India is fortunately seldom directed at the players, it's usually either people fighting amongst themselves or, as in this case, against the police. The crowd started breaking up chairs and making bonfires in the stands. Fortunately the stands were made of concrete and could not be burnt. The only other wooden thing in the stadium that would burn was the scoreboard and so that was set on fire too. In one section of the stand metal chairs were thrown about. This was dangerous, and people began to panic and rush from the stadium. People were being trampled on; outside the stadium the shops were burnt and looted. We were told to go upstairs to our rooms and the metal gate at the top was locked to ensure our safety. People crowded up to the gate laughing and joking and generally giving us the raspberry. They didn't seem to mean much harm but Bruce Taylor ('Tails') wasn't leaving anything to chance and started throwing buckets of water at them. Each time he threw a bucket of water they would try and back down the stairs but they still got drenched nevertheless. They appeared rather to like this treatment. Eventually we managed to attract the attention of some of the police and indicated there were some people whom we wanted dispersed. One policeman arrived at a most inopportune moment, just as 'Tails' was emptying one of his numerous buckets of water in that direction. The policeman was drenched, and it said a lot for his good humour that he did disperse the crowd for us.

The Indians seem to revere their film stars. The Nawab of Pataudi, who was captaining the Indian side at that time, had his wife Sharmila with him. She is a well-known actress in India. Many seemed to be quite as interested in her as they were in the cricket. People would stay behind for quite some time to see her leave the stadium.

This was a very low-scoring match which we came so near to winning. The Indians were left with 268 to win and we felt that they would have to work very hard to get these runs. With the score at 76 for 7 and two and half hours of play remaining our chances could hardly have been better, then suddenly a thunderstorm hit us. This storm had been hovering in the background for some time, but because it so seldom rained we had not taken much notice of it. I thought everyone in India must have had their prayer mats out because sure enough this cloud came over the top and we got the lot. Although it only rained for a matter of twenty minutes or so the damage was done and the ground was virtually under water.

It was frustrating to be so near victory and to see how inefficiently they tried to cope with the conditions. They

53

were rather slow in taking out the covers which were ground covers. When the rain eased women were sent out with buckets and large pieces of cloth and they proceeded to mop up the water that was lying on the covers and wring it into the buckets. We thought this was certainly an inefficient way of doing it. We wondered why they did not lift up the covers, get the water away from the centre, and dump it somewhere in the outfield. This looked feasible to us but they didn't seem to see it that way.

Graham Dowling was naturally terribly keen to win this test as it would have been the first time we'd beaten India in a test series. He went out in bare feet with a stump in his hand trying to drain the water away. He also tried to get the rest of the team to help but, as it was, there was really no hope at all. We just had to accept it and that was that. This match marked the end of the Indian section of the tour. Things were never easy in India, and sometimes trying, but I found it fascinating and, miraculously, none of us had got ill.

In India we did meet some real characters. Naga was one. He was a bearer (we would call him a waiter) in Hyderabad. He served in our dining room and he never seemed to stop smiling. There were only two teeth in the whole of his head and these were both in the front. When he smiled they looked like fangs. We asked him how many children he had. 'Well, saab, I had eleven, but two died, so I have only nine at the moment.' To us he didn't look very old, certainly not old enough to have nine children. We asked him how much he earned doing the job as a waiter and if it was enough to support his family. He said, 'Well, saab, I get 150 rupees a month,' which was about £8 sterling. We said, 'Only 150 rupees a month! How do you manage to support all those children on that amount?'

'Ah ha,' he said with that familiar smile again, 'Sometimes I get tips.'

I remember Bob Cunis having him on.

'Naga, my good man, we never seem to get the best part of the bird, do we? Are you sure we have the best pieces out here?'

54

'Oh yes, saab. Oh yes.' said Naga.

'Surely this thing here looks like a crow,' Cunis carried on.

'Oh no, no. It is definitely chicken, saab.'

He kept repeating the phrases, 'I get for you saab, I get for you,' and, 'don't mention it, don't mention it'. When he handed us something, the boys would always say 'Thank you, Naga,' or show some appreciation and he would always pipe up with a 'don't mention it'. I remember Bob said to him once 'Look, Naga, if we thank you for something there is no need for you to say, "don't mention it".'

'Don't mention it, saab, don't mention it,' said Naga instantly.

'Look Naga, don't say that because we mean thank you when we say thank you. There is no need for you to say "don't mention it",' said one of us.

'Don't mention it,' repeated Naga for the hundredth time. At that point we thought we had better accept it. On another occasion one of the boys was banging the salt shaker on the table. We always had difficulty getting the salt out of the shaker because of the humidity in the air. While it was being banged on the table, we suddenly heard a shout from the kitchen, 'I get for you, saab, I get for you.'

I sometimes wonder how many children Naga has now, and I hope he still sometimes gets tips.

5

New Zealand v. Pakistan, 1969–70

Our itinerary for the tour of Pakistan was to take in the main centres and in general our accommodation was far better there than it had been in India. We often stayed in Inter-Continental hotels or others of similar standard. We started the tour in Karachi and although the city was near the coast there was virtually no greenery to be seen; in fact, when coming in to land everything looked so dry and arid we could have been flying over a desert.

As soon as I got to my hotel room in came a waiter with water to drink and as usual I asked for the old reliable Fanta. He went away and came back with the drink and then, when about to leave, he put out his hand for a tip. This surprised me for in India, although the people hope for tips they hardly ever ask, being more inclined to look out from the corner of their eye when leaving in the hope that you might call them back.

The first test match in Karachi was drawn, and then we went on to Lahore in the Punjab, the land of the five rivers. Here it was green and pleasant with lots to see. The Mohammed Ali mosque, for instance, is quite magnificent. I didn't play in the first two tests; the main reason given by the tour selectors was that they wanted as many runs as possible off the new ball before the spinners came on, which was very often after as few as four overs had been bowled. It seemed to me to be a daffy idea, to be overreacting to the situation. At that point I simply wasn't a middle order batsman, and there was some irony in the fact that, when Graham Dowling opened in Hyderabad in India, he managed only 14 runs in the morning session. My argument was that if I wasn't good enough to open I shouldn't

57

be in the team. I think it can be established that except in the case of one or two New Zealand players, my scoring rate in test matches over the years has compared quite favourably with that of my fellow batsmen. Anyway, the selectors were vindicated in one way (and I got over my hurt), for we won the second test at Lahore by five wickets, and I was as pleased as everyone else that we were one up in the series.

Our victory in the second test appeared to cause the Pakistani selectors to panic somewhat. Before the series began Mushtaq Mohammed had been flown home from England where he had had a very good county season. So too had Younis Ahmed, and I think these two were their leading players. But largely as a result of this loss in the second test the selectors left Younis and Mushtaq out of their side for the final test in Dacca. We felt the selectors had done us a big favour here and we rubbed our hands together with gratitude.

An irritating event took place at one official function in Lahore. One speaker spoke for most of the time in Urdu, the Pakistani language. I couldn't understand why this was necessary; it would have been no less appropriate if our manager had reeled off a list of Maori place names, something I believe has been done before by more than one New Zealand sporting side.

From Lahore we went up to Rawalpindi, the original capital of Pakistan. A few English people still live in Rawalpindi and we were even able to drink some English beer in an English-style pub.

The wicket prepared in Rawalpindi for our match against the President's XI was easily the best we played on in Pakistan and India. A lot of runs were scored at a very good rate, Bruce Murray getting 157 of our first innings total of 357 for 3 declared.

Javed Burki had been brought back and asked to captain their side. Javed had previously toured New Zealand and had also spent quite a lot of time in England, attending Oxford University. He brought his wife along to the game but unfortunately the crowd, for reasons unknown to us, were not fond of Javed and apparently were swearing at him rather crudely during the day's play. Javed said later that it was probably the last time he would bring his wife along to a game.

As the wicket was so good, and it was only a three-day match, there was little chance of a result and with two hours of play remaining in the match things began to happen. The crowd, who had been growing more and more restless, started to riot, throw chairs, and fight among themselves. Then they started to advance on to the field, at which point we decided it was time for us to leave. I couldn't help thinking to myself that at such times, when there is absolutely no chance of a result, when one side is just blocking out time, perhaps this was not such a bad way of ending the game. It would, of course, be madness to encourage this sort of thing, and I wouldn't like the chaps who sit in Section Thirteen behind the bowler's arm at my home town's ground at Carisbrook, Dunedin, to get similar ideas.

Immediately after this game we travelled to Dacca. The hotel there reminded us of certain experiences in India. It was my turn to room with Bruce 'Tails' Taylor. We went up to our room and sure enough the cockroaches were out in force, so off came the shoes and whack, whack, whack. 'Tails' of course was an absolute master at this. It wasn't long before we noticed the Inter-Continental hotel close by so we asked to be shifted next day to better accommodation just around the corner. The one night we did spend where we were was one too many because it gave a rat the opportunity to get into my cricket bag which I'd left open on the floor of our room. You can't help but marvel at some digestive systems for in the morning I found that it has eaten holes in my gym shoes and in the 'cigar' or soft finger area of my batting gloves.

Bryan Yuile had strained a muscle in his neck so I was brought back into the team for the third test. A considerable number of spectators turned up at the ground to watch us practise on the day before the third test. For a while they were kept back behind some closed gates, so at least in the early stages of practice we had some degree of privacy. Eventually, though, they broke through the gate and came crowding along. I was padding up when a hand appeared in front of

59

my face and I heard the familiar words, 'Baksheesh, saab, baksheesh.' It was a beggar asking for money. Once again 'Tails' was summoned and given the job of guarding our kit and encouraging the spectators to return to where they'd come from. 'Tails,' who is tall, wore big boots with long spikes on them; he definitely commanded respect, and at this sort of work he really excelled.

Fortunes fluctuated a lot during the test match. I made a century in the first innings and Mark Burgess, aided by the gritty Bob Cunis, made a match-saving undefeated century in the second. Coming to the final day it looked as if Pakistan had a very good chance of winning so the beating of drums, the blowing of whistles, the chanting of songs got even louder and louder. The spectators became so excited that our boundary fieldsmen in particular began to have problems coping with them. 'Bag' Murray is normally cool and calm, almost a laconic sort of a fellow, but on this occasion he did get annoyed when they started throwing things at him. Pieces of fruit were thrown at him and in the end he was hit by, of all things, a banana. This was the end as far as 'Bag' was concerned and he hastily decided to come in from the third man boundary to show the umpire the evidence, and to complain in the hope that something could be done to put a stop to it. But while this was going on Dayle Hadlee, oblivious to what was happening, was running in to bowl. Graham Dowling was fielding at mid-off and could see that 'Bag' was fast approaching the wicket, so he called out to Dayle to stop his run-up to the wicket. Dayle didn't hear him. There were a couple of us in the slips who knew 'Bag' was coming but we had to return to concentrating on our jobs as Dayle was getting closer and closer to delivering the ball. He let go a nasty one which gloved Asif in front of his face. The ball flew towards the vacant third slip position. By this time 'Bag' had arrived on the scene and with banana in one hand, he dived and caught the ball with the other. We were in hysterics, all the more so when he rolled over and held the ball up claiming the catch. Some of the boys were saying that this was just not on, that Asif had been put off by 'Bag' calling out as he closed on the wicket. So it was generally agreed that Asif could not be given out. 'Bag' was not put off by this in the slightest. He ran very quickly across to the square leg umpire and thumping the banana into his hand said, 'Well flop me! Look what has been going on out there.' 'Bag' never swore of course, he made do with the word 'flop'. 'Bag' didn't get very far, however, as there wasn't much the umpire could do with 40,000 screaming people, so play simply went on as before.

Later the crowd got the impression that we were deliberately slowing things down. When we went in for afternoon tea, which followed shortly after the 'banana' incident, I felt the atmosphere was such that it would have been a good idea if an announcement were made explaining that, irrespective of the rate we were getting through our overs, we would still have to bowl twenty overs in the last hour of play. This might have quietened most of them down.

I don't know how the others felt, but I was getting edgy as this crowd seemed more violent than any other we'd played in front of. For the first time, it seemed to me, it looked as if they could focus their attentions on us rather than keep to fighting among themselves. As we walked off the field, 'Bag' went over to the policeman sitting at the entrance to the tunnel to ask if he could do anything about the commotion. The policeman merely shrugged his shoulders. I didn't blame him either, for if the police had gone out on the ground it would probably have provoked them further. A spectator just above the tunnel threatened 'Bag': 'Don't you waste any time, man, or I will get these people to riot.' For a change I was looking forward to our cup of tea.

At tea Pakistan were 40 for 2, but straight after the break they lost a further two wickets to be 46 for 4 and it began to look as if we had a rough chance. In the meantime a very large, black and angry cloud was looming and it seemed certain that it would rain. It appeared that everything was going to happen at once. The crowd again started to throw things and to fight among themselves. Then chairs were thrown and at this a few people panicked as they were being pushed down the aisles in the stands. The stands were two-tiered and people were being pushed from the upper to the lower tier. The only chance spectators had of escaping this was to come out on the field which is what happened. At that stage we ran for cover.

There are two schools of thought on how one should leave a cricket field in such a situation. Some say you should get off as quickly as you can, and others that you should walk off without hurrying because by running off you might just stir the crowd up that little bit more and so make matters worse. I found that if you did make to run then people would run at you and try and trip you up. So although it requires steely nerves I'm inclined to think it is better to walk off at a brisk pace, and look out for yourself. The stumps are always grabbed, for self-defence, but that takes care of six fieldsmen only, leaving the other five and the two umpires to fend for themselves. In Dacca nobody was hit as they left the field, and except for the odd pinprick in the backside or the leg nothing upsetting happened.

When we eventually found our way inside it was obvious that there would be no more play, so we stayed where we were with a guard on the door until the crowd had dispersed. The Dacca police were rather better 'equipped' than any of the others in India or Pakistan. Not only did they wield long bamboo sticks very effectively, but they also had helmets and shields. We sat and fidgeted for quite some time before it was finally decided to bring the bus up as close as possible to the dressing room door. From there we were to walk to it very quickly and be whisked back to our hotel. When we emerged there was still a crowd of people milling round and the police had to make a path for us. We walked through the crowd with trepidation. It was a tense, uncomfortable situation and one felt as if something foolish and dramatic could have occurred at any time.

Right through the tour our clothing, particularly that made in England, was much sought after. Several students came round to our hotel asking if we had any clothing or cricket equipment we wanted to sell. One member of the side, who shall be spared identification, had run short of money. As he wanted to buy some things in Dacca, and since his clothes had been beaten

62

on the rocks while being washed for the last two and a half months, he had no hesitation or compunction about disposing of them. While some of the items he sold were in reasonable condition, some of the underwear and socks were not. They had holes in them as if they'd been in a bomb blast but he still managed to sell them and the extra few rupees he made were put to good use. Many of us considered that the socks were quite capable of walking off after their new owners.

In the summer of 1970 I returned to England and had my best season for Worcester scoring ten centuries – a county record. In February and March 1971 we played two tests in New Zealand against Ray Illingworth's M.C.C. team. In the first test at Christchurch we lost by eight wickets with Derek Underwood running through us on a turning pitch. I managed to get 76 in the second innings. The second test at Auckland was drawn but at one stage we looked close to our first victory over England. They were saved by two fine innings from Alan Knott.

WORCESTER v. WARWICKSHIRE AT WORCESTER 2nd, 3rd SEPT. 1970
G. M. TURNER 133 NOT OUT

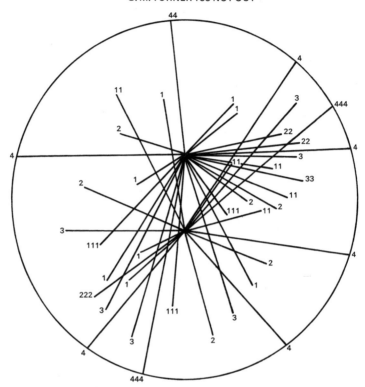

10th Century of the Season (Worcestershire Record)
133 runs in 276 mins. from 244 Balls

1st Day 19 no in 46 mins. (36 Balls)	14 Fours
	8 Three's
2nd Day 50 Runs in 139 mins. (96 Balls)	13 Two's
100 Runs in 236 mins. (201 Balls)	27 Singles
50 Partnership with J. A. Ormrod in 93 mins.	**133 runs**
50 Partnership with T. W. Graveney in 35 mins.	
100 Partnership with T. W. Graveney in 80 mins.	

Runs Scored off Warwickshire Bowling
D. J. Brown, 41 Balls – 22 Runs
N. M. McVicker, 35 Balls – 25 Runs
K. Ibadulla, 44 Balls – 18 Runs
L. R. Gibbs, 80 Balls – 30 Runs
W. N. Tidy, 24 Balls – 24 Runs
J. A. Jameson, 20 Balls – 14 Runs

6

New Zealand Tour of the West Indies, 1972

Like most of the New Zealanders I was looking forward to a tour of the West Indies but I was soon to discover that most of the impressions I'd been given were false. The image I had was of sun-drenched islands covered in palm trees; calypsos, the surf running on beautiful white sandy beaches, magnificent swimming and hordes of happy smiling West Indian faces wherever one went. Only in one or two places did this description almost fit; for the rest a very different picture emerged.

The first paper I picked up on arrival in Kingston, Jamaica, carried a story of a bank robbery that had just taken place. Two passers-by had been killed in the robbery. A road block had been set up to stop the eight robbers and they had been machine-gunned down as they tried to crash through the barricade. They were all killed.

I thought, 'Hell, what's this place?' We were 'advised' not to go out after dark unless we were accompanied or in a group. We were fortunate in that we were staying in the area called New Kingston which is one of the so-called better areas of town. Nevertheless, we took this advice, though our presence in numbers didn't deter the many prostitutes from propositioning us, when we were strolling down to the nearest pub.

We had our first practice at Sabina Park. There was fortunately no shortage of ground bowlers and this saved our pace bowlers some work. It is difficult for them to last through a full two-hour session in a hot country. One of the characters on the ground I remember quite well. His name was 'Sleepy' Williams and he had apparently been around for years, though no one quite knew how old he was. He bowled leg-breaks and googlies, and he bowled them pretty well. We were told that one of his joys was that he had bowled Sir Leonard Hutton when he had toured there with the M.C.C.

We played our first game in the West Indies against Jamaica. Apart from learning that the wicket was very good and that it was going to be difficult to get other sides out, there wasn't a lot to remember the game by. From my point of view my batting disconcerted me. I spent about an hour at the crease and found that I was missing full half-volleys and generally playing particularly badly without really knowing why. My judgment was so bad that I felt like a tenth-grade club player. I couldn't understand it, it was as though I had lost my natural ability. Fortunately, I was to improve very soon after this bad knock. All I can put it down to is the fact of acclimatising and also being a little bit out of breath because of the heat. I found that I was puffing and blowing so much it was difficult to concentrate, and as a result my judgment was poor.

From Kingston we went across to the other side of the island, to Montego Bay, for our match against the President's XI. Montego Bay is better known as a tourist resort, in particular an American tourist resort, although it's now very popular with Canadians as well. The ground there was not nearly so good as Sabina Park, Kingston. Montego Bay is much smaller than Kingston and not many people were expected to come and watch. It was very rural indeed. The game soon became a one innings affair, again because it was such a good wicket. About ten days would have been needed to get a result. I scored my first double century there and as it was so early in the tour, and I was not fully acclimatised, I played myself into the ground. At times I just defended for a while to get my breath back and bring myself round. Bruce Taylor said to me afterwards that he could see some vultures circling above, and at stages it must almost have come to that.

The West Indian test team for the first test at Kingston was to be announced after the match. It was here in Montego Bay that we saw the first signs of just how parochial people are in the West Indies. There doesn't appear to be much unity in West Indian cricket. Each of the major islands is represented on the West Indies selection panel and it seemed to us that

66

whenever a test was to be played on the local selector's island he endeavoured to get as many local players in the team as possible. The other selectors, realising this, tended to give in to the selector concerned knowing that their turn would come later. I realise this remark could be strenuously denied but nevertheless that is the over-riding impression we gained. When you look at it from this aspect you can see that this can be one of the points in favour of touring sides playing the West Indies at home. The advantage they have of playing under their own conditions can be cancelled out if they don't always play their best side against you.

Seven players, Joey Carew, Charlie Davis, Lance Gibbs, Roy Fredericks, Vanburn Holder, David Holford and Grayson Shillingford had already been selected and had arrived in Kingston. We thought that these seven were certain to play but the selectors surprised us by deciding to leave out Vanburn Holder and instead bring in the local player, Uton Dowe. Although we thought that Dowe was quite a useful performer we did not think he was quite as good as Vanburn Holder whom I know well because we both play for Worcestershire in England. It also seemed certain that a younger batsman would be brought in as they were known to be desperately look-ing for one at that stage. It was common knowledge that the choice was between Lawrence Rowe and Alvin Kallicharran and it was no surprise to see Rowe selected as he was the local from Jamaica, while Kallicharran was from Guyana. I don't for one moment believe that this was a bad selection, because Rowe, who has the unusual habit of whistling each time he plays an attacking shot, is such a good player and proved it during the series, but knowing the way politics were in the West Indies there seemed to be little doubt about whom they would choose.

Uton Dowe had provided problems for us in the match against Jamaica and although he was quite a short fellow he bowled at a lively pace. He was able to get the ball to skid on to you very quickly from a reasonable length, sometimes from even short of a length, and this meant that if you were on the back foot too often the ball was apt to hurry through low and trap you lbw or bowl you. Graham Dowling had difficulty with him in the early stages, whereas I was able to overcome most of these problems by leaning on to the front foot. Unfortunately Graham got trapped very early in his innings and was not able to correct it in this particular game.

Before the match our friend 'Sleepy' Williams came up to me in the nets and gave me what I thought was sound advice. He said, 'Beware of Dowe'. He sounded suitably sinister. 'He is not as easy as he looks. And watch out for his bouncer. It skids on to you very quickly.' This was exactly right, and anyone who tried to hook him got into difficulties. He did not have the normal kind of bouncer which tends to balloon a little. Although it was pitched very short it skidded through at throat height – very useful indeed! The attitude of the crowd rubbed off on the players and tended to encourage bouncers. I am sure the bowlers felt an obligation to whistle a couple around the batsman's ears each over.

It was in this test match that I played one of my more valuable knocks on the tour. I batted through our first innings of 386 to remain not out 223. Ken Wadsworth and Hedley Howarth really fought and gave great support. When I was just short of the 200 mark Hedley Howarth joined me and Uton Dowe attacked him, showing no mercy and not restricting his short-of-a-length bowling in any way. Hedley got hit a couple of times on the body, so I went down to him in between overs and said, 'Look, Hedley, I'll take Uton. So just back up at the end of the over and I will try and keep the strike.' But he wouldn't have any of this and asked me to play normally as he thought he could handle him. Hedley also thought that as long as Dowe bounced them at him the worst that could happen was that he'd be hit. My experience of tail-end batsmen in the past had been that in general they were cowards, particularly the fast bowlers. Although they enjoy handing it out they certainly don't like receiving it. I was surprised by, and full of admiration for, Hedley that day. As an observation I'd say that bowlers are usually the hardest people to satisfy with equipment. Hedley is no exception in this respect. I have seen him pick up fifteen or twenty different bats and state that not one of them was to his liking.

From Jamaica we went on to Antigua in the Leeward Islands. We arrived early in the evening and were shown to our hotel which perched on a hill overlooking the harbour where a couple of cruise ships were anchored. Antigua relies on tourism a great deal and a passenger ship docks at the harbour almost every day. However, the people were not very friendly, and in fact there was a distinct anti-white feeling on the island. Antigua was the first place where I was called a 'honky', a rather general and bitterly derisive or acrimonious term for a white man.

It was here in Antigua that Graham Dowling really began to have serious trouble with his back and although I was to be rested I ended up having to play in the Leeward Islands game as Graham decided at the last moment that he could not play.

From Antigua we travelled to Tobago, a beautiful little island not far from Trinidad and very near to the South American continent and Venezuela. We were down to play a two-day match there and it was decided that Bevan Congdon and I would have a rest. This was actually decided before we arrived in Tobago even though one or two of the boys suspected a conspiracy, alleging we must have had prior knowledge of what the island was like. We stayed at the Mount Irvine Bay Hotel, quite the most beautiful hotel we stayed in on tour. It had a magnificent swimming pool with concrete stools built in it up to a bar, so that you could sit in the water while drinking. A very dangerous life style!

It was here, in Tobago, that we met Colin Cowdrey and the Duke of Norfolk who were on holiday. Colin had had a rough winter in England and was recovering from an illness, and he thought the best place to spend a fortnight recuperating would be in Tobago. Colin is a keen golfer and the hotel's golf course is easily the best I've ever seen. The grass on the fairways was lush and springy and thickly textured. The course was so good that the professionals had played on it in a T.V. series of the Rest of the World v. the United States.

Colin was very helpful in discussing the West Indies side and the tactics that the English side had used against them on their previous tour. We took an avid interest in what he had to say for at this point I think we were averaging about two wickets a day and this was becoming rather demoralising. It looked as though we could never hope to bowl them out. Colin agreed that they had experienced similar problems when they were in the West Indies. He said it was depressing to look through their batting list when they were four wickets down and to see that there were still world-class players to come. It was really a tail between the legs attitude. There seemed to be no prospect of ever getting through them all. His advice, though hardly palatable, was the only one he could give: to keep on and on and there may just come a time during the series when things would go our way a little and the break would come. If this happened any time then he felt they might go to pieces a little. When this did eventually happen in the series, in Barbados, we let the chance slip away from us. Tobago was, in marked contrast to Antigua, a very friendly place and the winning of the two-day match, even though it wasn't a first-class game, was good for morale.

The seventh match was against Trinidad at Guayacara Park, Point-à-Pierre, the game resulting in the inevitable draw.

After the Trinidad match we moved to Port of Spain to prepare for the second test and our first look at the Queen's Park Oval. This was easily the best ground for spectators that we played on in the West Indies. It holds nearly 30,000 people, whereas most of the other grounds have a capacity of between 12,000 and 15,000, which is not enough to cope with the numbers wishing to watch. The outfield was quite smooth and well grassed but unfortunately the pitch was one of the poorest we came across. Everyone felt that here was the place which offered more chance of getting a result than anywhere else in the Caribbean.

Once again we lost the toss and Gary Sobers decided to put us in to bat first. We did not mind this because although there did seem to be moisture in the wicket we thought it might go to pieces later on. As long as we could get through the first morning and the period immediately after lunch without losing too many wickets we thought we would be in a good position to dictate terms. Things went well for the West Indies in the first session,

70

and out of only a handful of balls that did anything off the pitch, two of them took wickets. Graham Dowling and I were both caught round the corner by Joey Carew off Sobers and we were 16 for 2, but a great innings from Bevan Congdon and fighting knocks from Bruce Taylor and Bob Cunis pulled us through.

The treatment Lawrence Rowe received from a section of the Port of Spain crowd was disgusting. Here was a young player who had just made a double century in the first innings of his first test in Kingston, and another hundred in the second innings of the same match, coming out to play in only his second test for the West Indies and the crowd booed him all the way out on to the park. The game of cricket alone is quite deflationary enough to the ego without this sort of thing. I just could not believe my ears.

This once again emphasised the parochialism that is rampant in the islands. I was told later that Rowe had not scored many runs in Port of Spain before this match, but this was no justification for such treatment. Again the match ended in the seemingly inevitable draw, though the advantage was slightly in our favour.

If I wanted to live in the West Indies, Port of Spain is where I would settle. Although it is not as glamorous as Barbados or as picturesque as Tobago, it is only half an hour's flight away from Tobago. I found it a rather more sophisticated and attractive city than any other in the West Indies. It is comparatively hilly so there are several splendid views and by night the city is quite beautiful. The beaches are not good, at least they weren't then, the water being noticeably discoloured by the discharge from the Orinoco which flows in from Venezuela just across the bay. Trinidad is one of the islands in the West Indian group that has some natural resources with oil coming from San Fernando and, as it is one of the largest islands, cropping is important and a lot of sugar cane is grown.

We were all looking forward to our visit to the island of Barbados because we had heard so much about it. Some said it was like a little England. The entertainment in Barbados was certainly well organised, no doubt because they rely solely on the tourist industry. The island is hardly large enough to allow the growing of much sugar cane. The local rum, Mount Gay, is something special. The locals informed me that one goes through three stages of drinking rum. First you mix it with Coke, then with ginger ale, and finally with water. After that I suppose you *could* drink it straight. I reached the second stage of drinking it with dry ginger and it slid down rather easily. I fear for anyone who let their enthusiasm for Mount Gay run away with them!

On the afternoon of our free day the team went for a cruise on a yacht. It was one of the best outings I have ever experienced. We dropped anchor a mere five to six miles from Bridgetown and just off-shore. There was plenty of drink, rum punch and a magnificent buffet lunch. If you wanted to swim you simply dived off the yacht and it was an easy matter to reach the shore. It was on one of these trips that Freddie Titmus lost some toes when he was trying to get into a small launch. We were fortunate that nothing like this happened to us, but I can remember diving off the yacht when a young women who'd just gone in ahead of me surfaced and yelled, 'Watch out! Jellyfish!' I was in mid-air when I heard her yell and I wanted to turn around and return to the safety of the yacht. It's said that Jesus Christ walked on water. Well, when I hit the water I went very close to doing just that. As it happened there was only one jellyfish to worry about. I missed it so there were no worries.

Once again the ground at Bridgetown, Kensington Oval, was a little disappointing. After all we had heard about cricket in Barbados we were surprised at how small the ground was and at how much potential accommodation space had been wasted due to the fact that one entire side of the ground had no stands, terraces or any other spectator facilities at all. In fact the place looked so rural that you almost expected to see sheep or goats grazing. Near the main pavilion there was a stand with a wooden floor. During the game, when the crowd got excited, they would rhythmically bang the bottoms of bottles on this wooden floor. After a couple of hours of this din, it started to irritate us and we began to wish that the floor had been made of concrete.

The crowd attendances too were very small even though I believe the islanders are tremendously interested in the game of cricket. In a way it was not unlike New Zealand, where a large percentage of those interested in the game don't really bother to come along. They either watch it on television at home or listen to it on transistors. I did see several people listening to their transistors while walking in the street and following cricket in this way.

The game against Barbados was the only game I captained and I broke our drought by winning the toss, but in so doing it almost cost us the game. It is a very brave man who puts a side in to bat in the West Indies, but on this occasion I wish I had because the wicket had a few hidden nasties. It looked much the same as the other wickets we had come across, and little did we realise that there was a lot of moisture underneath which was not visible from the top. For the whole of the first day the ball really bounced and moved, and we were fortunate that they had decided to rest Vanburn Holder because it was between test matches. I am sure he could have easily bowled us out in that morning session. Payne and Moseley, the Barbados opening bowlers, thankfully did not bowl straight enough on this lively pitch and did not make us play. I batted very badly myself, but was lucky in only having to play about two deliveries out of six each over. The mere fact that I stayed there for an hour was a slight contribution. With just over an hour and a half to play in the match Barbados needed only 136 runs to win and as the wicket had got better and better as the match progressed they should have walked it. But we bowled and fielded extremely well and came out of it with a draw, Barbados being 87 for 6 at stumps. We hadn't been anxious to be added to Barbados's already impressive collection of the scalps of touring sides.

We watched the preparation of the wicket for the third test match in Barbados very carefully. It seemed that it was being prepared in the same way as the one for our previous match against Barbados. It looked identical and so we decided that if we won the toss we would definitely put them in. This seemed to be our best chance. But once again we lost the toss and it came as a shock to us that Gary Sobers decided to bat on it. He had put us in for the test in Trinidad and there seemed every reason in the world that he would do likewise here. We found out later that the groundsman at the Kensington Oval was a comparatively new one and Sobers was unaware that the wicket had been playing quite differently. Gary had not seen us play the match against Barbados and so had no real idea of how it was going to play. For a change we were rather better informed than he was. Events proved our assessment of the pitch's probable behaviour to be correct for we bowled them out for 133. Almost as important was the fact that they took nearly all day to score these runs. It gave the wicket a chance to dry out before we had to bat on it. We followed this up with 422 runs and it looked as if we had our best ever chance of winning. But the West Indians fought off defeat by batting out the rest of the game, Charlie Davis making 183, and Gary Sobers 142. Hedley Howarth bowled an incredible 74 overs in the innings, taking 2 for 138.

After the disappointment of the Bridgetown test we moved on to Guyana. Helpful souls had armed us with the information that the method used for most of the crime committed there was choke-and-rob; this in contrast to Jamaica where guns were favoured and, presumably, more effective. Some of the more gruesomely curious members of the side were keen to view some of the fish known as piranha which feed on human and other flesh and are said to be plentiful in the rivers in Guyana. As it happened our programme was so full we had to forego this little delight.

The Bourda ground reminded me very much of an English ground. It was not large, once again holding about 12,000: but everything was very well organised. The outfield was similar to the ground in Port of Spain, Trinidad; well grassed and level, and the pitch was flat and very true. I have never played on a wicket with so little bounce. There was virtually no movement at all off the pitch either with seam or through spin. It was just too docile and slow so from the batting point of view, although it was very difficult to get out if you played down the line, it was just as difficult to score freely because of the slowness of the pitch.

We had capacity crowds every day. I was not surprised at this because not only were we told not to go out at night but apparently the locals did not either. Perhaps the cricket was a welcome substitute for a social life they lacked in other respects. The people certainly seemed to react strongly to the stimulation of being together in such a large group.

I doubt if I shall ever forget Georgetown, Guyana, for it was there that I scored 259 runs in successive innings – one against Guyana, the other in the fourth test. When I reached 200 in the test match one of the spectators came running out on to the field. This seemed almost traditional and inevitable whenever a player got to the hundred or two hundred mark. Sometimes, with any luck, they would also bring some dollars with them and slip them in your pocket. This was more likely to happen to a local player, unfortunately, but you would nearly always get a pat on the back and congratulations. This fellow came running out, with a typically West Indian floppy hat on his head, and when he got within about ten yards of me he stopped, threw his hat on the ground and started jumping up and down on it shouting, 'You no good bat! You no good bat, man!' At this I thought to myself that I did not have a lot to say to this gentleman, so I just turned away and tried to ignore him. But he carried on and on and from the side it probably looked as if I was ignoring a fellow who had come out to congratulate me on making my 200; but this was the last thing on his mind. I feel sure that he must have lost a lot of money on me when I got 200, because I noticed in the crowds throughout the day that a lot of gambling went on. There would be bookies at various points around the ground; in fact anyone who wanted to set himself up as a bookie could do so easily. They seemed prepared to bet on just anything. For example: who the ball would go to in the field next. I got the impression that a bet as to whether a player would reach a certain score or not could have been more substantial than the usual. This is all I can put it down to with this particular chap. In the end a policeman came out on horseback and ushered him off the ground pretty smartly.

It must have been a very disappointing match for the locals. It certainly was for us. Play was interrupted by some rain during the first two days and as a result the West Indies batted an hour into the third day before declaring at 365 for 7. Because they had batted so long there was very little we could do except bat on and on.

Very early in the game the crowd realised that there was little chance of a result, that this game was going to be another tame draw, so they became edgy. A large number of them had probably been looking forward to this match all year, and now it had come along and nothing really was going to happen to excite them. This fact I think had a great bearing on the rioting that was to follow: this, and Clive Lloyd's run out. Clive was making his comeback into test cricket, not having played any of the earlier test matches, and was going quite nicely. He was in his forties when Charlie Davis joined him at the wicket. Almost immediately there was a disastrous mix-up which resulted in Clive being run out. It was one of those run-outs where it is difficult to blame one player in particular but because Clive was a local player, and because he had just come on to the test scene once again, many people must have had money on him to get at least a fifty. As he left the field people started to lob a few bottles on to the ground. Once this started our boundary fieldsmen had to come in to the middle. Fortunately the park was too big for anybody to reach the middle with a bottle, unlike at Sabina Park. We waited there for some time while the bottles kept coming, and Bevan Congdon went out to the boundary edge to try to calm the people down. He really was taking his life in his hands because these people were not going to stop. He soon realised this as bottles kept landing all around him. He returned to the centre and the police came out and tried to clear the bottles off. Unfortunately one of them struck a policeman who in his rage, picked it up, turned around and threw it back into the crowd. This was the end; the bottle-throwing intensified and it became a contest between the crowd and the police. At this point we left the field for about twenty minutes.

76

In the meantime, Clive Lloyd had been asked to go up to the commentary box so that he could speak to the people over the radio. He pointed out that mix-ups and run-outs just happen from time to time, that Charlie Davis should be absolved and would they please settle themselves down so that the game could continue. This really was not a very good advertisement for Guyana because the rest of the West Indies were also listening to the commentary. We went out again but from then on it must have been very miserable for Charlie Davis because they were willing him to get out to every delivery bowled to him. The spectators yelled and carried on voicing their views of the incident. Bob Cunis told us afterwards that at the boundary he was offered considerable sums of money from different people if he could get Charlie Davis out. We all felt for Charlie and I think he was very glad when stumps were drawn not too much later. When he left the ground he had to leave through another exit because quite a crowd had formed outside waiting for him. The police escorted him to a waiting car and took him hurriedly back to the hotel. I believe that he had to stay in his hotel room and not leave it. They even had a guard at his door. He told us later that when he got back to Trinidad, a lot of people were waiting for him at the airport and assured him that they would get Clive and fix him as he was causing all the trouble. It looked as if the atmosphere for the last test match at Port of Spain could be uncomfortable.

There was a section of people in Port of Spain that thought they virtually subsidised West Indian cricket. Two of the tests were played there, their ground being by far the largest and best in the West Indies. They felt that they should not be subsidising West Indian cricket if the other islands were going to treat the Trinidadian players in such a bad way.

But to return to the last day of the test in Guyana. Things were enlivened a little when a branch of a tree on which too many people had been sitting outside the ground snapped. The paying spectators in the stands were highly amused. Our first question was 'has anyone been injured?' Keith Campbell came up with the reply that probably none would have been injured through the fall, but some might well have been eaten by the piranhas in the moat surrounding the ground.

The masseur in Guyana was quite a character and I spent a lot of time on his table in an effort to try and get some life back into me. At that time I felt that I needed the help of someone like Professor Barnard, not to give me a heart transplant, but a couple of new legs! In fact things were getting rather serious at this time because my cricket was starting to interfere drastically with my social activities. Throughout the tour many people had rung us up at our hotels and wished us every success and good luck and so forth. Guyana topped every other place for this: an amazing number seemed to want us to win. The reason given often enough was that the people were too racial in Guyana. Enthusiasm for the game was so great in Guyana (it couldn't have been anything else) that a prostitute in our hotel came up to me at the bar, after I had scored a few runs, and offered me her services free of charge. I gracefully declined.

After Guyana there was only one more game before the fifth and final test in Trinidad, and this was against the Windward Islands on the small island of St. Vincent. I was rested in this game which gave me the opportunity to look around and to mix with other people than just the cricketing fraternity. I spent some time with the head medical officer on the island, a Yorkshireman with the keen sense of humour so many of them seem to have. He showed me the island and also invited me to spend an hour or two with him at the Labour Party club rooms which served the indispensable English beer. He told me of the recent elections on the island, which had previously been governed by the Labour Party. In the elections Labour and the main opposition party, the People's Party, which had leanings (he said) towards Black Power and Communism, had both captured the same number of seats. Everything had hinged, therefore, on an independent candidate, formerly a member of the Labour Party, who had won a seat himself. This gentleman had decided to re-align himself with the Labour Party, but while I was at the club an announcement came over the radio saying that this gentleman had changed sides. The People's

Party had offered him the premiership and this was what he wanted. There was an uproar in the club, and it was embarrassing to see so many adults in tears. They all said it would be the end of St. Vincent, and my friend felt sure he would only be on the island for a couple of months or so more. He believed that the People's Party would either ask every white man on the island to leave, or strip them of any leading positions they held.

There was also quite a commotion outside on the street, but of a different order. Supporters of the People's Party were rejoicing and celebrating the victory. There was much gaiety with bands playing and drums beating.

The final test in Trinidad was to be played over six days. Once again Sobers won the toss and the West Indies totalled a substantial 368 in the first innings. This, coupled with the fact that it was a rain–interrupted match, put paid to any chance we had of winning the match, and in the end we had to struggle to avoid defeat. We could only muster 162 in our first innings but Sobers didn't enforce the follow on, preferring instead to go in again. They managed only 194, but even so this meant we needed 401 if we were to win. As it happened we staved off defeat mainly through the efforts of Bruce Taylor and Ken Wadsworth, who safely saw the last 106 minutes out to leave us 253 for 7 wickets.

So we were to leave the West Indies having drawn all five test matches, with neither side having been able to prove itself noticeably better than the other. A five-match series ending at nil all didn't offer much excitement for the spectators or joy to those who were hoping, and indeed expecting, that the West Indies would beat New Zealand and so restore some of their, at that time, sagging international standing. Several observers and critics found the series dull, and said so. We came in for some trenchant criticism, particularly from one or two West Indian critics, who endeavoured to place most of the blame for the negative aspects of the cricket on us. I'm convinced this was unfair. The wickets were, by and large, not conducive to producing results: we were nearly always chasing large first innings totals, and we lost the toss five times running. Sobers made no concessions, gave us nothing. We didn't expect him to. Nor, by the same token, could we have been expected to have made concessions. We would dearly have loved to have been more often in a position to take the initiative, but fate decreed otherwise. We were criticised for our slow over rate, and in spite of the fact that we were desperately short of bowlers, this criticism was largely justified – we should not have been as slow as we were. It would be a pity, though, if so much of the good cricket played in this series were overlooked because it was a drawn series.

What did disappoint me rather more was that we could not manage a result in any of the island matches, excluding the two-day game at Tobago and the one-day match at St. Vincent. There were two main reasons for this: one, the pitches were so good and two, we kept losing the toss and were nearly always chasing big totals. It is very difficult to win games if you're a long way behind when starting your first innings. People surely don't expect a side's batsmen to throw a match away simply because their bowlers have been unable to bowl the opposition out for a reasonable score.

Also, the attitude of the home teams did not lend itself to producing a result. Like ourselves, they do not play a lot of cricket, so when they do get the opportunity to play a first-class match, every innings seems to count so much more, especially when they're playing against a touring side. Naturally, several players were playing for positions in the West Indies side, and as a result they tended to bat on and on against us. Opposing captains were also reluctant to put their heads on the chopping block, because they could not afford to lose a match in front of their home crowd. Only someone like Gary Sobers, who is well established, could afford to play attacking cricket – and this is his natural way. The younger captains were reluctant to take a chance and maybe risk losing a game because they would then almost certainly lose their position as captain.

When we did manage to win a toss, against Barbados, I tried to set something of an example by declaring the New Zealand innings closed at lunch on the second day. Most opposing sides batted on for as long as they could, for up to two days if they were able to manage it, and in a four-day match there can hardly be a result thereafter unless the side batting second collapses twice.

Another disappointing aspect of the cricket scene in the West Indies, where interest in the game is so great, was the sad sight of so many people being turned away at the gate because of the small capacity of many of the grounds.

Although I scored heavily on the tour, I did not enjoy my successes as much as I should have. Before going out to bat the thought of scoring 200 runs in a test match is exciting. I found, though, that my first 200, in the first test at Kingston, Jamaica, did not give me anywhere near as much satisfaction and enjoyment as I had hoped for. It was not so much that the innings was such a drain physically and mentally, but that it had all gone towards so very little as far as the team was concerned. Certainly we saved the match, but that was about all. I don't mind grinding away (or at least I didn't then) for up to ten hours if in the end the side wins or goes close to winning, but on this tour whenever we went in to bat in an important match we invariably seemed to be chasing a big total. This gave us no alternative but to aim for a big score ourselves, and this in turn meant safety-first measures. No one was able to score fast so we became involved in endurance tests. One played down the line and waited for the bad ball.

I approached each innings by not thinking in terms of 200 or more, but by looking at it session by session. Fifty or 60 runs a session added up to around 150 runs for the day, and I found it essential to pace myself throughout the day. At the beginning of a session I would play myself in for a short while before looking to play in an aggressive manner. Then I'd look for drinks, which would revitalise me. After this, my concentration back again, I would look to play aggressively once more. It was all very mechanical but it seemed the only course open. The ideal is to bat fluently throughout an innings, yet I felt that if I tried to do this I would tire too quickly, and my concentration and application would desert me. I disciplined myself to conserve my energy and play defensively when I was tired. When I felt fresher I again became more aggressive.

This kind of self-discipline is essential if a batsman wishes to play long innings regularly.

Several centuries were scored in the series, but only one other double century, that by Lawrence Rowe. I could not see myself scoring double centuries in any other way than the way I went about it. If I had put all my energies into getting a hundred then I'd have gone flat and got out more easily. About the only way to have become fit enough to play aggressively all the time would have been to train like a marathon runner. But then I'd have had no time for batting.

I did become irritated with myself at not being able to master one thing: when I was not out at the close of the day's play I found it impossible to relax properly during the night and could not get a decent night's rest because of the strain imposed during the day. Towards the end of the tour I was prepared to try anything. In fact, in Guyana I deliberately drank a generous amount of alcohol early in the evening in the hope that this would knock me out so that I'd get sufficient sleep. All that happened was I'd wake up at three o'clock in the morning and toss and turn for the remainder of the night. A possible answer could be that cricketers should take up yoga or learn self-hypnosis.

After the fifth test we flew from Trinidad to Kingston, Jamaica, and from there to Bermuda. We had one final game in Bermuda before the boys flew home to New Zealand and I to England to rejoin Worcestershire for the coming season. Bermuda had become Americanised: the people spoke like Americans, and they thought big. They referred to our three-day match against them as an international test match.

The game was played on grass for the first time in Bermuda. The wicket was 'lively', to say the least, and it looked as though they'd put far too much marl on it. Bermuda had a left-armer playing for them who had apparently played against the 1965 New Zealand touring side. His name was Clarence Parfitt and he was virtually unplayable on the matting strip on that occasion. He bowled left-arm around the wicket, cutting his hand across the ball and getting it to lift viciously and angle towards the slips. Actually we might as well have been playing on matting, for with the fourth ball of the first over that he bowled to me he decided to try dragging his hand across the ball to see what would happen. The ball flew past my right shoulder. More by good luck than good management Terry Jarvis and I managed to put on 145 before being separated and the side was all out for 249 runs. This was sufficient for us, because we bowled Bermuda out twice by the end of the second day and won by an innings. All that was left was to say goodbye to the rest of the New Zealand side and turn my thoughts towards the coming English season.

As I left for England and Worcester I felt enormous relief that the tour had ended, that I did not want to return to tour the West Indies for quite some time. I felt I needed to recuperate, almost to convalesce. I should hate to be an old man and be asked to tour the West Indies.

7

English County Cricket

I arrived in England for the 1972 season on the second day of
Worcester's game against the Australians. I really did not feel
like going through a full county season, and I was certainly not
prepared to play the same way as I had in the West Indies.
But this was easier said than done, for in the very first county
match, against Somerset, I batted through the innings to be
88 not out at the end. Thereafter, though, and for the remainder
of the season I decided that I was going to play a lot more
shots and the runs I did get would be scored as quickly as
possible. I was certainly not going to spend hours and hours
at the crease.

It is a strange fact that though, from time to time you get
very tired playing cricket (and at this stage I had every reason
to be) you don't necessarily need a rest to bring yourself round.
I had been suffering from mental fatigue, a common state
for a cricketer, a state far worse than physical tiredness. Here
I was back in England still playing cricket seven days a week,
yet I began to feel much fresher and started playing better
than I had ever played before. Since then I have noticed that
for a few weeks I can feel a little bit flat and all of a sudden
I come right for some reason unknown to me. Perhaps this has
something to do with the life you are leading away from the
game. If you are enjoying good company, leading a pleasant
social life, and are able to relax fully off the field, then you are
bound to feel more relaxed when playing. It's difficult to find
the real reason, but one factor about cricket in the United
Kingdom that I'm sure is relevant, is that the conditions vary
so much that the game can hardly ever be dull.

There are many characters involved in cricket, and it is the presence of these characters, plus the little misfortunes and sidelights which occur on and off the field that make the life of a county cricketer so interesting. Sometimes it is a particular individual's misfortune that we all laugh at. For example, Worcester were playing our wicket keeper Rodney Cass's old county, Essex, down in Chelmsford, when one of the Essex batsmen tried to hook, got a top edge, and skied the ball. It went straight up, many a mile. Rodney had been 'keeping quite well, and when a ball is skied anywhere near to the wicket it is always the 'keeper's catch. With those large web-like gloves, how can you miss? As soon as the ball went up Rodney yelled, 'My ball!' We all stood back as good lads should and watched him first of all whip his cap off, then run round in a circle as he took off one glove and threw it to the ground. Having thrown one glove away it must have gone through his mind that it would be difficult to catch the ball with only one glove on, so he threw the other off as well. So there he was, left with just his inners on; he might as well have tried to catch it with his bare hands. After going through 360 degrees he ended up by diving full length without even getting a touch on it! Although it was to his and the side's misfortune everybody had an uproarious time over it. So much for the dour reputation of county cricketers.

In the same season, when we were playing Somerset, Roy Virgin, who had been doing particularly well for them, came out to open the innings as usual. He'd walked about ten yards out on to the park before he realised that he didn't have his bat with him, so he had to turn round and return to the pavilion to get it. This was very embarrassing for Roy, and very amusing to the spectators and other players. He eventually rejoined his partner, took guard at the wicket, and promptly shouldered arms to the first ball he received. The inevitable happened; it knocked his off-stump over. Why did he bother?

County players are not the only characters. Some umpires also fall into that category and, like the players, they also appreciate relaxing whenever they can. Quite often you can have a chat to the square leg umpire if you happen to be fielding near him, as long as you keep quiet when the bowler approaches the wicket to deliver the ball. Likewise when you're batting. Once you are established I see no harm at all in exchanging a few words with the umpires now and then. In fact I consider it very important to find some way of relaxing between deliveries, and this is one way of doing it.

One of the better-known umpires who has appeared on the umpiring scene in recent years, and one who has provided the players with a great deal of entertainment, is Harold Bird. Of course with a name like that his nickname has got to be 'Dickie'. Dickie was a good cricketer himself, although he was very nervous and for this reason he didn't do quite as well as he might have done. An example of how this nervousness was apt to show itself occurred, so the story goes, before one match in which he was to play for Leicestershire against Lancashire at Old Trafford. Dickie, as an opener, knew only too well that the opposition had a fairly quick bowler. When the Leicester skipper went out to toss Dickie was seen to disappear into the lavatory. When the skipper came back after tossing, Dickie yelled from the security of the lavatory, 'Have we won the toss, captain?'

The skipper replied, 'Aye, Dickie, lad.'

'What are we doing?' asked Dickie.

'We are batting, Dickie, lad; you'd better get your pads on.'

He said, 'Oh Christ!' shut the door and spent another ten minutes in there.

Dickie's mannerisms on the field and his signals for boundaries are unique, and at times hilarious. He was umpiring a match at Guildford, in Surrey, and while he was standing at the bowler's end, the striker hit one high in the air. Dickie sensed very quickly that the possibility of a six was on. The ball was hit towards mid-wicket and Dickie took off after it, sprinting out towards the boundary. The ground at Guildford is fairly narrow so Dickie was really quite close to the edge by the time the ball just dropped over for six. He raised his hands triumphantly high above his head and with what seemed great elation signalled six runs. I could not think of another umpire doing this sort of thing. Goodness knows what Dickie Bird would have done if the ball had fallen short and had been returned to the wicket. I dare say he would have sprinted back to a position where he would have been able to make a decision on a run out if necessary.

While standing in another match, he moved so quickly in an effort to get into a position square of the wicket at the non-striker's end that his feet went from under him and he ended up flat on his face. If he was put off he didn't show it: he remained at full stretch on the ground and gave his decision from there which, on that occasion, was 'out'. By-play apart, Dickie Bird has proved himself to be a very fine umpire. He was added to the test umpires' list in 1973 and did a test with New Zealand and two with the West Indies, and proved himself to an able umpire at this level as well.

In February 1973 I was back in New Zealand and we played three tests against Intikhab Alam's Pakistan side. The first at Wellington was an even draw in which I got two 40s. In the second match at Dunedin we were totally outplayed and lost by an innings and 166 runs. The third test at Auckland, though it eventually petered out into a draw, had several interesting features. Opener Rodney Redmond, playing in his first test, scored 107 and 56 in brilliant style – he has not played a test for New Zealand since. And Brian Hastings (110) and Richard Collinge (68 not out), coming together with nine wickets down and two runs needed to save the follow on, put on 151 – the highest last-wicket stand in tests. So we got 402 – the same as the Pakistan first innings. In tests I averaged 47.00, but a really big score eluded me and my highest score in the series was only 58. In the Plunket Shield season I managed 132 against Auckland and 131 against Wellington.

8

Limited-overs and First-class Cricket in England

Since I started playing cricket in England in 1967 there have been numerous changes in the game there, particularly in relation to the introduction of more limited-overs cricket – the John Player League (forty-over matches) began in 1969 and the Benson and Hedges Cup (fifty-five-over matches) in 1972 – as well as the introduction of the bonus points system in county cricket, and also variations to the rule on the covering of wickets.

Gillette Cup cricket was the only limited-overs cricket being played when I arrived in England. This competition, which began in 1963, features sixty-over knockout games, the bowlers being allowed run-ups of unlimited length but no more than twelve overs each.

In 1969 it was felt that, as the Gillette Cup had been so successful, there was a good case for another limited-overs competition. John Player came in on this in a generous way financially, and the level of sponsorship increased from £65,000 in 1971 to stand at £80,000 per annum in 1973. There is a prize of £50 for the winners of each League match, which is in addition to the following monetary prizes (included in the overall sponsorship figure) for the complete competition: Winning team £2,000; Runner-up £1,000; Third team £500; Batting awards £1,150; Bowling awards £1,150; Fastest televised fifty £250. Benson and Hedges, Gillette and the Prudential Company also provide generous financial support.

The general public had been crying out for more of this so-called 'instant cricket' and the John Player League was to provide it for them. In a Sunday afternoon's cricket the public are able to watch a game in which a result is assured.

The players' first reaction to this competition was that it would be bad for cricket. This was particularly so of the older men who had been playing three-day cricket for so long that it was going to be harder for them to adapt to the change. But as there was to be so much prestige and extra money involved for clubs if they did well in the competition, the players had to take it seriously and were forced to adapt to the new game. Most players adapted fairly quickly, discovering that one of the hardest things to do was to switch from a three-day match one day, to a forty-over game the next, then back to three-day cricket again.

It was interesting to note just how much the standard of one-day cricket improved as time progressed. Field placements became more sophisticated, and it soon became standard practice for only one slip to be used right from the beginning of the forty overs, and then after four or five overs to be moved to the outfield. He would either go right to the edge, at deep square cover, or on the boundary just forward of square leg in what we refer to as 'on the drop-kick'. So the orthodox field placement was changed to mid-off, cover, square cover, a man right out on the edge in the square cover position, and a deep third man. On the leg side, a deep fine leg, a man just behind the umpire, saving one, a mid-wicket and a mid-on. Later on in the contest, when the slog was really on, you would probably push your mid-on and mid-off quite a bit deeper and drop the man just behind the square leg umpire out to the edge of the boundary. This field placement sometimes varied of course, depending on who the batsman and the bowler was; but this was the orthodox field setting.

Now this obviously meant that a player was not going to score very easily by playing in an orthodox manner. A beautiful cover drive generally brought only one run as it was hit to the man fielding on the boundary and it became far more profitable to play an 'off-glance'. The object here is to get sufficient bat on the ball to beat the keeper and yet tickle it fine enough to beat third man. So for what was virtually a 'nick' you were getting four. Harry Pilling of Lancashire became an expert at this, particularly in running the ball to third man and taking a run early in the over so that it would allow one of their big hitters most of the strike. There were players in the Lancashire side who could hit the ball very hard indeed, such as Clive Lloyd, Faroukh Engineer, and David Hughes. The first object seemed to be for Harry to bat for as long as possible, right through the forty overs if he could, quietly collecting runs and wherever possible giving the strike to the bigger hitters. Nowadays it's not so easy to get away with this tactic as the third man is set much finer, almost behind where second slip would be, and the square cover is positioned further behind point to save the single from the ball that is run off the face of the bat.

When it gets down to the last ten overs, and if the opposition still has a few wickets in hand, then of course the field placements are vastly different again. At this stage there may be only two men saving the one on either side of the wicket, one at a squarish mid-wicket and the other at short cover. These two players block the push and run, while the rest of the players are brought in close enough to save the two (on an average-size boundary this would be about ten yards in).

During the first season of this limited-overs cricket a 160 to a 180 total was a reasonable score under good conditions. Today a side needs 200 plus. In 1972, against Warwickshire, for example, we scored 246 batting first and lost the game. We refer to these games as 'whacky races' almost from the outset, and this sort of cricket is a very difficult game for bowlers as well as batsmen. I think it has taught a lot of bowlers where to bowl when the slog is on, how to restrict batsmen, and what fields to set for them. It is generally accepted that one must bowl close to the batsman because you cannot afford to give him freedom of arm movement. A misconception that still holds too much currency in New Zealand and elsewhere is that the way to restrict scoring is to bowl wide of the stumps. If you do this a good batsman can virtually hit you to any part of the ground. The length of the delivery, too, is another vital factor. When slogging, a good length delivery can sometimes be quite easily whistled out of the park anywhere from about long-off to deep fine-leg. So a bowler who can master a block-holer or a yorker will certainly find that he will receive far less 'tap'. A yorker is not a very easy delivery to bowl and you only have to be a little short of yorker length and it can still be hit a long way. A yorker or a low full toss certainly can not be whistled out of the ground. This is the ideal delivery, particularly if it is bowled into about middle and leg stump.

Limited-overs cricket is not the ideal game for the older man, especially the fielding side of it. I remember Tom Graveney commenting that he doubted whether too many cricketers in the future would be able to play as long as he had been fortunate enough to do. There is just nowhere that you can hide somebody in the field in this type of cricket.

I feel that to play a cricket match of less than forty overs is to reduce cricket to the near farcical. But unfortunately, due to rain or bad conditions, these games are sometimes reduced to as few as ten overs. When it gets down to a ten-over contest, I am afraid all sense goes out of the game and it becomes more or less a laugh. It is a widely debated point whether leg-byes should count in these games because so often the ball deflects from the pad and has been killed to such a degree that even a close-in fielder struggles to prevent a run. I consider it is essential to allow leg-byes otherwise the bowlers would bowl into the pads all day long and this would tend to kill the game.

Forty-over cricket is devilishly difficult for the umpires and I sympathise with them here because they have so many rules to follow. In England, where it rains so often, and many games become reduced-over matches, the umpires have to take out their pens and pieces of paper. Also, when it comes to awarding wide balls, the interpretation of what is a wide ball and what is not is necessarily different in limited-overs games. It would be so easy for some bowler to take advantage of leniency by slipping a couple of deliveries down the leg side every over and because the number of overs is limited this is just not on. Umpires are strict here, and rightly so. I've played in matches where after two balls in a row have been bowled down the leg side in one over, the third one has been called a wide simply because it was the third in a row, irrespective of the fact that it had brushed the batsman's pads. This is the way it has to be.

In forty-over cricket it is vital to have a good wicket keeper for with all bowlers restricted to a maximum run-up of fifteen yards few can bowl above medium pace. Towards the end of the innings batsmen tend to charge the medium-pacers and it is important to have a wicket keeper who can stand up behind the stumps and prevent this from happening.

With the John Player League and the Gillette Cup firmly established most of us felt that we were playing sufficient limited-overs cricket, but in 1972 the Benson and Hedges Cup, fifty-five-over matches, competition started. Most sides approach these fifty-five-over games in similar fashion to Gillette Cup cricket, usually starting off with a field near to being orthodox, with at least two slips and a gully, but perhaps doing without someone catching around the corner on the leg side. The Benson and Hedges competition is played in the first half of the season and followed later by the Gillette Cup, the final of the Benson and Hedges being played at Lord's Cricket Ground generally about mid-July. It now has almost the same following as the Gillette Cup. In 1973 Benson and Hedges sponsorship stood at £80,000 of which over £15,000 was paid out in prize money.

The Benson and Hedges competition is made up of twenty teams in four zones – North, South, Midlands and West – and each team plays its zonal opponents once. The two top teams in each zone qualify for the quarter finals and the eight teams remaining go on to a straight knock-out draw on a national basis until two finalists remain.

Before limited-overs cricket became firmly established a bonus point system was introduced into county cricket in 1968 in an effort to make the game more attractive to the general public. Under this points system, ten points are given for a win, five for a tie but none for a lead on the first innings. In the first innings one point is awarded for every 25 runs scored over the score of 150 in the first 85 overs by the batting side. The bowling side gets a point for every two wickets taken in the first 85 overs. The bonus point system was altered in the 1974 season.

Changes to any laws of the game are never easily accepted

by the players. We look upon such changes with an extremely critical eye, but I think it is fair to say that this system of scoring points was quite well received by most. The only flaw in the system, which was exploited by a couple of teams in the early stages of the competition, was the awarding of one point for every two wickets taken. These teams usually declared with nine wickets down, thereby robbing the opposition of a bonus point. But this tactic was short-lived. In 1973 the bonus system was amended to make it possible to get two further batting points in the early stages of an innings. You can get an additional point if you score at least 75 runs in the first 25 overs and another by bringing up 150 runs in 50 overs or less.

While limited-overs cricket has affected county cricket in numerous ways I feel that it has been mostly beneficial. Players are more aware of the need to speed up the game; it has improved the overall standard of fielding and brought about noticeable alterations in field placement. Seldom before had a man been seen on the deep square cover boundary or the deep forward square leg boundary to seam bowling. I remember only too well in 1968 and 1969 that if a side was left with more than 100 runs to score in the last hour (bravo for the introduction of the compulsory twenty overs or more in the last hour's play) even with six or seven wickets in hand, it was considered too many. Today, however, under good conditions a side can often expect to score between 120 and 130 in the same time.

I know from the personal angle how much limited-overs cricket has developed my play. Even as an opener one had to accept that shots had to be played from the outset, and I rather surprised myself at the number of shots I was able to play, shots I would never have attempted had I not been put in that situation.

Limited-overs cricket has resulted in a reduction in the number of first-class games. In 1969 the number of county matches decreased from twenty-eight to twenty-four. Again in 1972, with the introduction of Benson and Hedges, they were further reduced to twenty. There was a strong school of thought which favoured that they be reduced even further to only sixteen matches, so that it becomes a fairer championship with all teams playing each other only once. Personally I would not like the number of first-class games to be reduced further for as it is the ratio between first-class games and one-day cricket is already a little bit lopsided. Those that believe in reducing the number of games to sixteen generally add that they would like to see those games played over four days, while others feel that, as so few people are coming to watch the three-day matches, to make them four would decrease the numbers even more. I don't think it would, because those people who come to first-class matches now are the really staunch supporters of the game and I don't think they would be put off by an extra day. In fact, more people might be encouraged to come as they would be more likely to see real rather than manufactured results.

To play four-day cricket in the United Kingdom would necessitate the full coverage of wickets. In order to get wickets to last for four days they would need to be on the green side for a start with a little bit of moisture in them so they would do something earlier on, and in the latter stages of the game take considerable turn. Uncovered wickets certainly make for varied conditions and this is one of the things that adds to the greatness of the game. But surely in a place like England, atmospheric and other conditions varying as they do, the condition of the wicket is inevitably going to change over four days. I contend there would be quite enough variation without subjecting players to the continuing hazard of playing on uncovered wickets. Injuries are accepted as inevitable in all games but with uncovered wickets things can get to the ridiculous stage.

With uncovered wickets there is more chance of a result (and this is what the crowds want), but do they want to see games finishing by the tea-break on the second day? I can remember the Worcester supporters seeing just this happen to us at home in two games in a row. In the first match Gloucester scored 265; then because of over-night rain we were bowled out for 58 and 88 runs. In the very next game Leicester had reached about 200 with a couple of hours left when the day's play was stopped by rain. It continued to rain in the night and in the morning they took one look at the wicket and immediately decided that they would bat on and get as many as they could before putting us in while the wicket was still wet. They scored a further 50 runs in about an hour and a quarter, having been fortunate to have had wickets in hand overnight. Then they proceeded to shoot us out for 40 and then 169. Not only were we bowled out and defeated so quickly in front of our home crowd, but Mike Procter and Graham McKenzie were dangerous; there is no other word to describe their bowling under these conditions.

It is argued that one of the reasons for the decline in the standard of the English test side over the past two seasons has been the excessive amount of limited-overs cricket and the limiting of first-class cricket. I certainly feel that four-day cricket would provide English players with a chance to prepare themselves better for test cricket; we must surely be providing enough of 'instant cricket' for the general public now. Yet while the amount of limited-overs cricket being played is part of the reason for the fall off in the standard of the English players it is only a small part. There is no denying that the large number of overseas players in county cricket has limited the opportunities available to young English players, and that this has curbed the development of a strong English side. On the other hand, the presence of overseas players has raised the standard of cricket, so that the locals who are playing are able to play in a better standard of cricket. The overriding result though has been that England has assisted other countries by providing such a good standard of competition for outside players. By making this available they have virtually cut their own throats when it comes to test cricket. A good example, of course, was the 1973 test series against the West Indies. Virtually all of the West Indian side were players who were playing in English county cricket. There really is an astonishingly large number of overseas players playing in England who hold regular places in their county sides. There are, I think, (and I exclude the many others who are on county staffs and who are in and out of the first side and still trying to make the grade) eighteen

Turner, with Hedley Howarth and Derek Underwood behind him, walks off the field after carrying his bat through New Zealand's second innings in the Lord's test

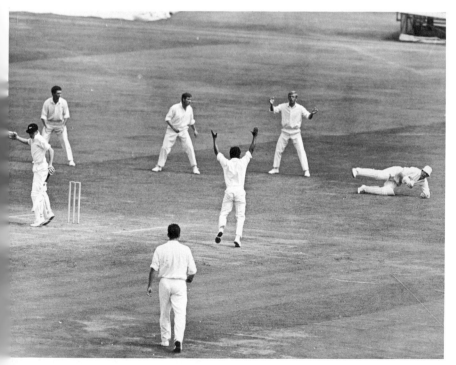

Murray (Middlesex) appeals for a catch but Turner survives. An incident from the New Zealand 1969 tour

A batsman in full command. These four photographs were taken during Glenn Turner's innings of 153 for New Zealand against the M.C.C. at Lord's in 1973. In the bottom left picture he is hitting Jackie Birkenshaw for six

Colin Cowdrey shown at the completion of a cover drive. Colin's restricted follow-through might appear to have lessened his power but because he was in complete control of the shot and his timing was so good a longer follow-through was not necessary

Tom Graveney driving a wide delivery from Johnny Gleeson (Australia) during the fourth test, England vs Australia, at Headingley, Leeds, 1968. He's done well to get to it, and while he's certainly got plenty of bottom hand into the shot the full extension on to the front foot and his poise stand out

West Indians, seven Pakistanis, four South Africans, four Indians, three New Zealanders and two players from East Africa. Yorkshiremen, of course, still believe that they do not require to go outside the bounds of their county, let alone outside the shores of the United Kingdom to get their players.

An important point in favour of four-day cricket is that it would make it much easier for all players (and this would obviously assist in strengthening the English side) to adapt to the playing of five-day test cricket. There is too much of a difference, aside from the obvious time angle, in approach and attitude between three-day and five-day cricket. Although there are a great many overseas players in English county cricket I don't think that increasing the number of home-grown players is in itself necessarily going to lift the standard of the English side. There are still well over 100 English players playing first-team county cricket and this ought to be enough to produce a top-class side. Australia has a first-class competition involving five state sides only and this seems nearly always sufficient to provide a strong side.

To sum up, I think overseas players have a definite and valuable place in county cricket: they help to keep the standard high and to draw crowds, but it is reasonable to restrict their numbers. The recent curbs will have the effect of doing this. So I would opt for the introduction of four-day cricket, full coverage of pitches and one complete round of sixteen county matches only. Here you would cut out four matches but gain, overall, four more days of first-class cricket. The number of one-day matches could remain as they are.

9

The Benefits of Sponsorship

The introduction of sponsorship on a large scale has revitalised cricket in England and provided money that was desperately required if the game were to retain its appeal and prosper. The old school of thought was that a game should be able to pay for itself by its gate takings, and although a few other games still manage to do this, in cricket it was becoming increasingly difficult to make ends meet. It is still far from being out of the woods, but things are more healthy than they were a few years ago. Certainly one-day cricket has brought back the crowds and heavy sponsorship has been the means by which we have been able to play so much of the one-day game. In recent years few people have been able to afford the time to go and watch the three-day first-class games. Common sense must tell us that the people who can afford the time are mostly older people and pensioners – this group far from makes up the bulk of potential spectators.

If the game of cricket were to die in the United Kingdom (a remote possibility indeed), it would certainly upset many people, for although there are not large gates at the first-class games there is ample evidence of a wide following through the newspapers and on radio and television. Sponsors have gradually become accepted as a necessary and legitimate part of the game. I believe that the reason for the Prudential Assurance Company deciding to sponsor cricket was that they had taken a survey which showed that a large proportion of those investing money with them came from the working class, so they felt that by associating themselves with cricket they might be able to bring their name in front of a different section of the community in the hope of perhaps winning their custom. The Prudential company sponsors one-day international matches of fifty-five overs per innings and provides £26,000 in sponsorship money and £4,000 in prize money.

The Test and County Cricket Board and the various counties themselves have been actively engaged in exploring as many avenues of fund-raising and sponsorship as possible in recent years, with considerable and gratifying success. While financial backing for cricket in New Zealand has grown also in recent seasons it is still lagging well behind the rate of increase in England.

If New Zealand cricket is to improve then the first thing that needs to be done is to find some means of increasing the amount of first-class cricket that is played. There is little point in a New Zealand cricketer looking to England for playing opportunities now, for the door is virtually closed. When a vacancy does become available now a player, to stand a chance of getting in, not only needs to be a test player, but a top-line one as well. Therefore, the only possible way open for a New Zealand player to gain considerable experience is to become a regular member of the national side; to play Plunket Shield cricket only is not enough: the number of games is too limited.

The New Zealand team's programme in recent seasons has been very full and this has helped to build a reasonably experienced international side. Unfortunately though, due to a variety of circumstances, we have lost the services of a number of these players and we are again in the position of having to rebuild much sooner than we ought to. This rebuilding process will take longer than most other countries, I believe, unless we restructure our internal cricket. I feel we should extend the Plunket Shield competition to two rounds – we would then get ten games or thirty days of cricket which would put us on a par with Australia. At the moment we do not play enough cricket for either spectators or players to become deeply involved. Cricket is probably the leading summer game in New Zealand yet we play so little of it. Often the result of the Plunket Shield series is a foregone conclusion after three games.

The introduction of further sponsorship would be the best and perhaps the most feasible way of seeing that more cricket is played in New Zealand. As an inducement to sponsors it is imperative that cricket associations and local bodies be prepared to see things from the sponsor's point of view and ensure that they are given their money's worth. Seemingly small things like being prepared to allow them to have their name over the Tannoy at the ground and allowing them to put up posters around the ground if the sponsors wish to do this. These things are important, and as long as it's not overdone the press and radio announcers ought to be free to use the sponsor's name occasionally. When all things are considered I think that sport ultimately benefits and is not degraded by its involvement with and support from advertisers. Surely there is scope in New Zealand for sponsorship on a scale relative to that which takes place in the United Kingdom? Looking for sponsorship is not begging for money; I can't see that Benson and Hedges and John Player would be spending £80,000 each a year unless they felt they were getting some return for their money.

I don't think it's entirely fair to judge the interest being taken in a game by the number of spectators present at the ground. While it is true that cricket does not draw very large crowds to most first-class games there is considerable interest in the results of matches. Most of our first-class cricket is played over the holiday period, around Christmas and the New Year, and wherever you are, on the beaches of Nelson or North Auckland, you can hear broadcasts over transistor radios. I am sure there is a worthwhile opening for someone to sponsor cricket in a big way in New Zealand. Rothmans, who are already involved in sponsoring nearly sixty sports in New Zealand, are well aware of the benefits to be gained from sponsorship.

Administrators can only do so much to help the game and the rest is really in the players' hands, particularly the captains. They must endeavour to play entertaining cricket. It appears to be in our nature to think first of not losing, before thinking of how we might win. This has a stultifying effect on the entertainment value of the game. It is the captain who must set the example and indicate to his side how he wants the game played. There are times when it is necessary to give your

101

opponent a chance to win in order to give *yourself* hope of a victory. When it comes to declarations, which sometimes have to be made even though they are not the most satisfactory way of getting results, it's mostly reasonable to give yourself a sixty-forty chance over the opposition. If they really play well, and you don't, they may end up winning. So what? There has been a damn good game of cricket and the spectators and players will have enjoyed it. I don't think that this is a soft approach at all because once you have decided how you are going to play the game, then you play it hard and give it all you've got. If you are outplayed then you must accept it and hope that next time you will play better. This is where the game is more important than the individual.

In the 1972–73 Plunket Shield series I was playing for Otago against Auckland at Eden Park. We batted first and totalled 276, to which Auckland replied with 387 for 8 declared. By batting on for as long as they did Auckland left us with virtually no chance of winning the match. This may have motivated Gren Alabaster to bat on longer than he would have normally, our second innings ending at tea time on the last day for 340. Gren was injured so I took over the captaincy.

When Auckland came out after tea, it was obvious they felt there was absolutely no chance whatsoever of them getting the 230 required for victory. I felt that there was no chance of a victory to either side unless they could be induced to go for the runs. We needed points badly to give *ourselves* a chance to get further up the table in the Plunket Shield. So I encouraged them by putting virtually everyone around the bat and giving them runs. When they realised I was giving them a chance they responded and took the opportunity. As it happened we could not bowl to a field, they batted very well, and they deserved to win. Quite naturally I was criticised for not bowling Bevan Congdon or Carl Dickel, but I felt at the time that they would have been given as much 'hammer' as anyone else. I might have been wrong, but I don't see that this, in yet another of those 'manufactured' three-day matches, mattered all that much. In any event the crowd at Eden Park, and there were 8,000 of them, were sent home happy and *this* was important. I believe it would have been criminal to let them sit there and watch two hours of boring cricket at the end of the match.

Our dressing-room scene was very depressing afterwards. Our boys were so down about the fact that we had lost. If we played more cricket then perhaps it wouldn't be so important for us not to lose. More cricket would help us to come to terms with this sort of thing, and I am sure we would play better cricket as a result.

10

Marriage

I suppose very few people would disagree with the statement that the most important decisions one has to make in life are choosing a wife and finding a suitable occupation, and that neither decision is easy to make. But for a Westerner to decide to marry a Sikh is very rare and difficult to arrange; mainly because of the problems involved in breaking down certain longstanding barriers.

I met Sukhinder, my wife, when I toured India with the New Zealand side in 1969. I remember only too well how difficult it was to see her. We met first at a cricket function but thereafter only on rare occasions because she was never allowed out at night, except when her father, who is a navigator with Air India, was away from home, when she would literally sneak out. One day, not realising that her father was home, I rang her place and he answered the phone. I asked if I could speak to Sukhi, to which he promptly and bluntly replied, 'Why?' It seemed lame to be unable to say more than, 'I would just like to talk to her.' He then asked who was speaking, so I identified myself and explained that I was in India touring with the New Zealand cricket team. He said that his daughter was not allowed out and that was the end of the conversation. I didn't feel that this was leaving me much room for manoeuvre.

Sukhi later disclosed that he had told her that people who travelled as much as I did had a girl in every port and going out with me was definitely not on. I think he probably sensed that things could become serious and he didn't want this to happen. Indian custom is such that it is vitally important for an Indian girl, in particular, to marry not only an Indian but also a man from her own sect. If she does otherwise it is often considered that she has brought dishonour on the family name. As it happened another female member of Sukhi's family had married someone of another religion and done just this. But for a daughter to become involved with someone from beyond the shores of India was almost unheard of and quite impossible!

Fortunately Sukhi was sent abroad to study, to college in Bethany, a small centre fifty miles south-west of Pittsburg in America. This made it possible for me to stop off on my return to New Zealand from England and on the way back to England as well. And during the 1972 tour of the West Indies her vacation time coincided with our stay in Barbados so she came down to visit me there.

The Gill family spends two or three months in Britain from May to August each year, and with Sukhi accompanying her parents I was able to see her in England also. Our meetings, though, were cloak and dagger affairs and we kept them a closely guarded secret. After three years at Bethany College, Sukhi graduated with a B.A. in History and then came to England, where once again her family was staying. It was at this point that a decision had to be made one way or the other because I felt her parents were going to hustle her back to India.

I shall never forget my first meeting with her parents which was during the first test match at Trent Bridge, Nottingham, in 1973. Although they were staying in Hounslow, which is between central London and Heathrow airport, I had a free Sunday during the test, so I was able to travel down to see them. The minute I walked into the room I could see I was on trial. Her father stood up to greet me, and seated all round the room were the relations the Gill family were staying with. Although he and I tried very hard to make conversation, there were moments when I could hear the clock ticking. I could see his point of view and why he was concerned for his daughter. For example, he didn't want her to become a casualty of the high divorce rate in Western society. Somehow I had to convince him that I was reliable and could be trusted – difficult to do, and although Sukhi and I had decided to get married at some time, our plans were very loose. Her father, though, lost no time in getting down to asking me exactly when we planned to get married. So then and there I had to draw my fixture list out of my back pocket and see when I could fit it in! It definitely had to be before I joined Worcestershire as I wanted Sukhi to come with me to Worcester. The only dates I could see free were right at the end of the New Zealand tour and before I went to Worcester. I even allowed for the possibility of Worcester getting into the Benson and Hedges Cup final which was just as well because they did. So I arranged that we would get married on the Monday and keep Saturday free in case of the Benson and Hedges final. I was going to have to play for Worcester on a Sunday in Surrey anyway.

As the date drew nearer and Worcester had won their way through to the final, I suddenly realised that if the game was rained off on the Saturday it would mean coming back to complete it on the Monday. This could have been tricky because Sukhi's father was not actually living in London at the time and was to make a special trip of a few days for the ceremony only. I thought that if rain did interfere with the play then I would just have to dash off sometime on the Monday and get someone to marry us very quickly. Thankfully my nerves were spared as we did complete the Benson and Hedges final on the Saturday.

I had booked to be married in a registry office in Brentford, near Hounslow, and I kept it a secret from the rest of the New Zealand team because I felt that if it leaked out I might have too many people around, particularly the Press. I had already experienced enough of that after scoring 1,000 runs by the end of May (see Chapter 14). So the only members of the New Zealand party that knew of the wedding were the manager, Jack Saunders, skipper Bevan Congdon, our Press man, Dick Brittenden, and our radio announcer, Alan Richards. I would have liked all the team to attend but for 'security' reasons it was too risky.

At first I had no intention at all of going through with a Sikh ceremony, but on talking to Sukhi's father again the day before the wedding he asked me if I would go through a small ceremony in a temple nearby in Southall. I explained to him that I couldn't hope to understand the significance of what was

107

going on around me and I hoped he didn't expect me to. I said that if it was important to him that there be a Sikh ceremony then I would go through with it. He assured me that it would be a much shorter ceremony than any I could expect if I were in India so I thought it would be best if I got it over and done with in England. Once I'd agreed to go through with it I was given some instruction. It is necessary to cover one's head before entering a temple and he suggested I either wear a turban, which I could set on my head like a cap, or a handkerchief. He also hinted that as a handkerchief would tend to drop off on occasions, a turban would be more suitable.

When we got to the temple I had to put on the turban and remove my shoes. I went in with Sukhi's father and she followed me with her mother and friends and relatives behind them. We all sat down in front of the holy book which they call the 'Grant Sahib'. The women sat on one side and the men on the other. In the corner two Sikh gentlemen sat behind a little drum called the *tabla* and a microphone and a harmonium. They started singing in Punjabi in the very high-pitched voices which characterise the Indian way of singing. When the singing stopped the holy man sitting behind the holy book began to read from it. At this stage I felt a cloth around my shoulders. Sukhi's father had stood up and draped this cloth over my shoulder and into my lap. Sukhi held on to the other end. I didn't know what this was for until later. The only thing I knew was that we were to walk round the holy book four times; everything else, they assured me, would be explained as the ceremony proceeded. When the time came to stand up and walk round the holy book, which was on a platform four yards by three, each of the male relations of the family stood at intervals around the book indicating that they were there to help us on our way through life. I wanted to walk quickly and get these four laps done in a hurry, but this would have been improper as it is traditional to walk slowly. In true male chauvinistic style I did enjoy the fact that Sukhi had to walk about three paces behind me. I held one end of the cloth and she the other. It was as if I were dragging her along. For some reason I couldn't help thinking of the days when man was reputed to have knocked his woman on the head with a club and dragged her off by the hair. After completing one circuit of the holy book we sat down again and there was more singing and more reading from it. This part of the ceremony was repeated four times. On completing the fourth round rose petals were thrown at us from behind and then came a very pleasant surprise: I saw a five pound note in my hand and one put in Sukhi's hand. I looked up and saw it was her father. Following him another relation put a pound in each of our hands and everyone who was there did likewise. I thought to myself then that I should have invited the whole team! In fact everyone in London should have come along. This had been a good morning's work!

With the ceremony over we all went to look for our shoes. I searched and found that mine were missing. In accordance with tradition the female relatives had hidden my shoes and the only way I could get them back was to give them a pound each. I tried to tell them that all I had was some change in my pocket, but they were not having any of that.

Once I recovered my shoes, I asked my father-in-law if I could remove my turban. But he wanted a few more photos. By this time I was on the street and was beginning to feel self-conscious wearing it, even though there seemed to be mainly Asians living in this area. When I finally went to take it off, I took it off the way one removes a cap when one has just had a victory in a cricket match. I went to launch it but fortunately I did not let it go. Apparently it is an insult to throw a turban. It really is terribly easy to do the wrong thing when marrying someone of a different culture.

The Sikh ceremony took only three-quarters of an hour and from there we went straight to the registry office a couple of miles away where I had arranged for my friends to be. The registry office wedding was rather anti-climactic and after some food and drink at Hounslow I returned to the hotel and told the team what had happened. We still had one more official function to go to, and that was a visit to Buckingham Palace. Although I had met the Queen and the Duke before, I had never been to Buckingham Palace so I was interested to have a look around. I felt I'd had a rather novel day, what with visiting Buckingham Palace and getting married twice in the same morning. After such a day I felt truly international, a little unreal, and in many ways totally blasé.

11

Short Tours: Cricket for Fun

At the end of each county season there are a number of short cricket tours abroad, usually of about a fortnight's duration. They are good fun and I have been lucky enough to be invited to go on a number of these. It is a good way of seeing places one would not otherwise see in the normal round of cricketing tours.

When I was still qualifying in England in 1967, Worcestershire had arranged to go on a trip to Ireland in mid-June and I was selected for this tour. It was here that I played my first game for the Worcestershire first XI in a two-day match against Ireland in Dublin. We spent four days in the city amongst some of the friendliest people one could ever wish to meet. Our hotel was superb, and so was the conducted tour of the Guinness brewery on the last day; as it was our last day we were told that we could drink as much as we liked. Unfortunately at this stage we only required topping up, so we were unable to take full advantage of the opportunity.

At the end of this 1967 season, Worcestershire was invited to play in Holland so we travelled to The Hague to play All Holland. The tour was organised along similar lines to the visit to Ireland; two days of cricket and two days for sightseeing. The weather this time was far from pleasant, and with few of our side having encountered matting wickets before, we found it a struggle to hold our enthusiastic opponents to a draw. Socially it was a tremendous trip. Before returning to England we were transported around the canals of Amsterdam, and spent a refreshing time in the Heineken brewery. Amsterdam was really alive at night, the restaurants and nightclubs seemed to stay open all through.

The game against All Holland was, for me, quite a novel experience. Basil D'Oliveira came to join me at the wicket. I think he had had a rather heavy night out, and in those days I was struggling away, collecting one run here and a couple there. One of their bowlers said in Dutch, after he had bowled me a full toss, 'I could bowl him six full tosses in an over and he would not hit me off the square.' Basil, being able to speak Afrikaans, which has many similarities to Dutch, understood exactly what this fellow had said and he replied. 'Well you just bowl another bloody one and see what happens.' This embarrassed the bowler and his team-mates because they had thought they had the big advantage of being able to say what they wanted without us understanding.

In Holland it is common for soccer and cricket to be played on the same ground, and sometimes you have to wait for the soccer teams to come off the field that you are going out to play on. The outfield on such grounds tends to have long grass and this makes it very difficult to hit a four along the ground. To overcome this the Dutch players had a skilled knack of chipping the ball over the inner field and getting two runs as a result. In the early stages of the game we thought these were rather chancy shots. But they did it with such irksome regularity that we began to realise that this was the way they very effectively played under these conditions. They had a chap called Tony Bakker who played particularly well against us and was held in high regard in the cricket circles of Holland. We struggled during this match, and only just managed to hold our own on the first day, but on the second day Jack Flavell decided that he would charge in a little bit and see if he could knock the top off their batting. He made life rather miserable for the early batsmen because not only were we playing on matting over concrete, but we were also using two piece balls, and this helped make the ball really fly.

It wasn't until three years later that I played cricket in Holland again, this time with Colonel Norman Butler's eleven. The colonel was stationed in Germany in a place called Goch. Through his contacts we mostly stayed in the army messes during this short continental tour which included Holland, West

In the dressing room during the match against the President's XI at Montego Bay during the 1972 West Indies tour. *From left*: Glenn Turner, Murray Webb, Terry Jarvis, Brian Hastings. Sitting at table: Bevan Congdon and Graham Dowling

eft: Glenn Turner hits Bedi for four and brings his total to over 1000 runs before the of May, 1973. Above: Dressing room celebration with (from left) Dayle Hadlee, rd Hadlee, Glenn, Richard Collinge (obscured), Bruce Taylor, Rodney Redmond and Hastings

Batting with Brian Hastings in the second test against Australia at Lancaster Park, Christchurch, 1974. "I don't know what happened: the best one can say is that I survived."

The dismissal that brought the Lancaster Park crowd to its feet. Greg Chappell attempts to crash the ball through the covers off the back foot but only succeeds in edging the ball to Jeremy Coney at first slip. Richard Hadlee has already begun to appeal

. controlled shot into the cover field during the second test
ᴈainst Australia at Lancaster Park, Christchurch, 1974

e inevitable mob of young supporters racing out to congratulate me on scoring the
t of my two centuries in the second test against Australia at Lancaster Park. I'm doing   my
st to get as far away from the wicket as possible. I was out 4 balls later for 101

Dick Motz, one of New Zealand's finest ever opening bowlers, pouring a glass of wine in the dressing room after the defeat of Australia at Lancaster Park. Glenn finished not out 110

John Parker, Sukhinder and Glenn

Germany and Switzerland. We did not play in The Hague or in Amsterdam on this tour, going up closer to the German border to a place called Deventer. We went on from there into Germany to places like Berglen and Mönchen Gladbach. Drinks in army messes are very much cheaper than they are outside, so from the social angle most of us overdid it somewhat. The colonel was very keen to organise wine-tasting evenings. We had one of these in Berglen and tasted about twenty-three different wines. You are supposed to swill it around your mouth and spit it out in a large bowl on the side, but few of us bothered about spitting it out. The trip from Mönchen Gladbach to Geneva was a fairly lengthy one so we decided to spend a night on the way at a very pleasant spot called Cochem on the Moselle near Koblenz. Once again we had a wine-tasting evening in an old cellar where the local wine merchant was very enthusiastic about letting us taste his wines. I remember going into a bar in Cochem where all you could drink was wine – they did not sell beer and this was quite a new experience.

When we got to Geneva we found that we were to be billeted there. You don't often think of people playing cricket in Switzerland or any of the continental countries but wherever there are reasonably large numbers of English and Australian people they have built up their own teams and competitions. Our match in Geneva was to be only a one-day affair and the ground that we were to play on was used as an athletics ground. Alongside it was a railway line and if you hit the ball over it you were hitting the ball into France. Around the ground there was a running track and the local rule was that you had to hit the ball across it in order to score a four. There was one snag: between the edge of the grass and the running track was a three to four-inch high concrete wall. The harder you hit the ball against the wall, the further it came back into play, unless you got a lucky bounce and the ball jumped over the wall. The boundaries square of the wicket were very short, but were particularly long behind the wicket. Down either side there were jumping pits and if you hit the ball into them then it naturally stopped dead in the sand. The wicket itself was ordinary grass with matting laid on top of it. It was hardly level, in fact there was a large hump in the middle. If the ball hit on your side of the hump it tended to keep very low; if it hit on the upgrade it bounced! It became almost like obstacle cricket. For lunch we were to have an hour or an hour and a half, however long it took, because this was the most important part of the game. We were taken to a very nice restaurant overlooking Lake Geneva and were immediately served with enormous quantities of chips and steak and some beautiful red wine which slid down rather too easily. It was obviously their intention to make sure that we drank more than our share of it. By the time we had finished most of us were hardly in a condition to continue a cricket match, and at the time I was nearing my hundred. When we continued playing I found that instead of hindering my play the wine seemed to have helped to relax me and brought the best out of me. I got to around 120 and thought it was about time I surrendered and made way for somebody else. Before I did so I said to their captain, 'Look, you come on to bowl and I'll give you my wicket as long as you can fix me up tonight.' He said he would arrange this and proceeded to lob one up which I duly slogged straight up in the air. While it was in the air he yelled at me, 'The bet's off, the bet's off.' Sure enough they caught it and I did not get fixed up.

The following day we left Geneva and drove all the way back to the Hook of Holland, a distance of just over 700 miles, far too long a drive in one stretch. I am sorry that I have not been able to go on these trips since because my commitments have generally been fairly full. Norman is no longer in Europe, he is back in England in Harrogate. However, he still arranges trips abroad and they are always well worth going on. His organisation is so good that if you don't enjoy yourself on one of his trips it is your own fault.

In September 1972, at the end of the county season, an International Wanderers side was selected for a two-week tour of Rhodesia. The itinerary was quite a good one because we were to spend the first couple of days up at Victoria Falls. This was really the perk. Then we were to play a three-day match in Bulawayo against Rhodesia, followed by a one-day limited-overs match in Gwelo, a little place between Bulawayo and Salisbury. From there we would close with a four-day match against Rhodesia in Salisbury.

We had quite a good side, although we were to find out later that we did not have enough bowlers for at the end of the county season the quick bowlers are a little bit short of stamina. We had Brian Close as captain. The team consisted of Close, John McLean, Graham MacKenzie, John Jameson, Tony Greig, Jim Parks, Norman Gifford, David Green, Merv Kitchen, Basil D'Oliveira, John Edrich, Bruce Francis and myself. By looking at the side you can see that we opened the bowling with Graham MacKenzie and Tony Greig and used Basil D'Oliveira as our third seamer and had Norman Gifford as our spinner. With such a side Brian Close found that he had to get his arm over quite a bit as well.

The team was far from short of characters, and with two chaps like Brian Close and David Green in the side we were certainly going to compete with anything the locals could produce. I had had experiences of Close in England and I can remember playing against him in Taunton, Somerset. I hit one in the middle of the bat, when he was fielding in the stupid mid-off position, and it hit him flush on the shin. My first reaction was to say, 'Are you all right, Brian, lad?' He replied, 'Just get on with your batting, you can't hit it hard enough to hurt me, sunshine.' After that I heard that he believed that pain was only in the mind, so nothing was going to hurt him unless he *thought* it was going to hurt him. Brian is a supreme optimist whatever he's doing whether it be batting, bowling or fielding. Although he is far from being a very good bowler he certainly believes that he is. I remember him bowling in Bulawayo to Mike Procter who was going particularly well at that time and who is a very big hitter of straight sixes. He hit Brian for a couple of sixes which went right out of the park. Brian came up and tossed another one further in the air and he managed to get it to drift away a little. I was standing at slip so I could see it drifting away from Procter. Procter went down the wicket and I think he originally intended to hit it straight back over Brian's head but ended up hitting it over

115

extra cover instead because of the drift. This, of course, is a far more difficult shot to play and a far better one. It went miles over the boundary into a marquee that was sitting well back from the edge. Brian stood there with his hands on his hips and declared, 'Well bugger me! I did him in the flight and all.' In the dressing room afterwards he carried this one on. He could not believe how he had done him so easily and yet had not got him out. As far as he was concerned Procter was as good as out to that delivery. We managed to draw that game, the scores were: Rhodesia 476 for 7 declared and 148 for 4 declared. The Wanderers got 276 and 284 for 8. Really we just managed to hang on to save defeat.

From Bulawayo we travelled to Gwelo for the one-day match. Unfortunately we had assumed that in this one-day forty-over match the rules would be the same as those we played under in England. As a result Brian didn't bother to check with the umpires beforehand, and no one bothered to come to us. We were soon to find out that their rules were quite different from those we were used to, and in fact we were allowed only four or five players on the boundary and the rest had to be within thirty yards of the bat. The batting side was automatically awarded four runs for any no ball or wides that were bowled, *plus* whatever else was scored. If you hit a no ball out of the park you could end up with ten, not a bad hit. If in the opinion of the umpire you did have an extra man outside the thirty-yard limit, then he would shout 'No ball!' and that was tough luck for the fielding side, four runs automatically. Brian Close was irritated by this and commented, 'We've been playin' the bloody game for ages in England; we come out here, where they've just started playin' it and they think that they know all about it, and they make their own damn rules!' I couldn't help but agree with him. The no ball rule was also different; they were still using what we term 'the old no ball rule' where the back foot was not permitted to cross the bowling crease before the ball was delivered. Tony Greig had a lot of difficulty here because his bowling stride is so short that he virtually bowls from between the creases.

Off the field Brian Close was good value at parties with his

116

repertoire of tricks. One of his best, I think, was the placing of a glass of liquid, usually beer, which was about three-quarters full, on the top of his head. The object then was to drink the liquid without laying a hand on the glass. At first I thought this was impossible, that it was a good enough act just to balance the glass on his head, especially late at night, though Brian does have the advantage over most of us because he has such a flat crown on his head. He walked across the room to one of the corners, put his head up against the walls, and let the glass slide down between them and his head. Just in time he trapped the glass with his chin, bit it, tipped his head back, and down went the drink. We thought Brian was very smart. David Green was our speed drinker; we didn't meet anyone in Rhodesia who was able to compete with him in this respect so we had things covered from the party angle at least.

In spite of the shock of being unprepared for the rule variations, we managed to win the one-day match at Gwelo. Graham MacKenzie came in with two balls to go and five runs wanted. He hit a six and that was that. We went on to Salisbury to play the four-day match and Brian Close won the toss and put them in. It is common to put the opposition in at Salisbury as the pitch is known for its excessive amount of moisture early on. Brian was a good judge of the conditions as we initially had them in all kinds of difficulties with four batsmen back in the pavilion in quick time. However, because of our limited bowling attack they were able, once they'd seen our opening bowlers off, to settle in and eventually totalled 273. This was not all that good a score in a four-day match. We had half an hour in which to bat that evening but the light was poor and with Procter bowling it meant three balls only before we went off.

It rained very heavily overnight, but there were quite elaborate balloon-like covers at the park which created a vacuum of hot air over the strip. It seemed certain that no water would get on the wicket, but we were to get a surprise when we came out first thing in the morning, because this is exactly what had happened. We found it difficult to understand how all the surrounds could be so dry when the only wet area was the strip we were playing on. It was so wet that play was delayed for about three-quarters of an hour. We knew that batting on it would be very dangerous and with someone who could use it, such as Procter, it meant that runs were going to be very difficult to come by. This is exactly what happened. We prodded on for quite a while and managed to get just past the follow-on, to 124 for 8 before Brian Close closed the innings. We thought we might as well try and make use of the moisture in the pitch. We managed to take three wickets fairly quickly before stumps but when we came out the next morning the pitch had dried out considerably. They went on to score 374 for 7 before declaring. We thought we had done our job in a way because the main crowd was going to be there on the third day which was Sunday. The fact that we managed to avoid the follow-on meant that the game went on for a little longer so they were able to get that good gate on the Sunday. But then they left us with the ridiculously large total of 524 to win in a day and an hour's play. At this point the boys were not happy, not just because they had played us out of the game, but because the wicket had been so wet and well-nigh unplayable. I'm afraid we slogged out very quickly for 112 and spent most of the fourth day at the swimming pool.

The game did have its moments of hilarity and once again Brian Close was involved. I remember one of the boys saying to him in the dressing room after the rain had got on the wicket, 'Well, Brian lad, it looks as if you might have to take a few on the body today.'

Brian replied, 'Aye, it looks like it.'

'Surely if you get one on the head it must hurt. You must be a little concerned about that.'

Brian promptly replied, 'No, the only bloody difference is that it goes for four.'

On one occasion, when returning to New Zealand after an English season, I stopped over in Singapore to stay with a friend who was in the R.N.Z.A.F. there. He got me into one of these thirty-over matches which they play in the evenings when it gets a little cooler. In these games no one is allowed to score more than 30 runs and I managed to get my quota. We were playing against the English boys and my friend had not mentioned who I was because he felt they might have objected. My presence didn't do any harm as the opposition won anyway, but it might have soured things if they'd known who I was. Once again this game was played on a lively matting wicket and although I did tell them I wasn't a bowler at all, which by first-class standards is very true, I was given a bowl towards the end and got a hat-trick. There was so much bounce in the wicket that it was difficult for me to decide whether to bowl off-spinners or seamers. I thought I would bowl my Freddie Trueman stuff and as a result I was really fast and nasty. I was approached immediately after the game by a chap who had been watching. He said to me, 'I think you have a bit of promise there. Would you like to play for the squadron?' I quickly replied that it would be nice but I was due to go back home so there really was not much point.

Later I was able to fit in a game with the Commonwealth XI in Kuwait on the return trip to England. They had been touring Pakistan and were stopping over in Kuwait for just under a week on the way home. We stayed a few miles out of Kuwait in the English village of Al Ahmadi. The ground we played on was quite unusual for apart from the matting wicket over shale, the outfield was of a very fine shingly nature. You had merely to stroke the ball quietly and it would seem to gather speed across the outfield. Once the ball passed you in the field, you had no chance of catching up with it. Fortunately around the outside of the ground they had a little wooden barrier so the ball did not go off into the desert. I made 99 runs and had tremendous fun towards the end of my innings because of the sandstorm which was blowing right up the wicket. At times it was difficult to see and I kept hitting this leg-spinner up into the wind, the ball going up a long way before stopping and being blown back. There was a chap on the long-off boundary who was given a hard time. I think he dropped me four times before he eventually managed to grip one. I felt a little sorry for him: he obviously dreaded every moment I was facing the leg-spinner and I felt like giving him a cheer when he finally caught me.

119

12

My Approach to Batting

When I first entered first-class cricket my game was very much centred on as watertight a defence as I could engineer, and a belief that you would never learn to bat and make runs if you kept getting out early. By all means encourage a young player to play his shots, if those shots are well executed, but if you continue to encourage a young player, whose shot-making keeps getting him out in the twenties and thirties, *purely* because you are wedded to the belief that aggression is attractive to watch, then you are doing that young player a disservice and he is unlikely to become a top-class player. To become a top-class player you must score a lot of runs; and to make big scores you have to bat for a long time. Too many players are praised for their aggression when they should be criticised for their lack of discipline.

At the start of my career I rarely played anything I didn't have to, and because New Zealand bowlers spray the ball around more than the English county bowlers do I tended to score more slowly in New Zealand than I did in England. This seemed to puzzle a number of people in New Zealand, and to provide fuel for those interested in pinpricking and denunciation, those who were invariably concerned with making comparisons, based on my performances, between the standard of cricket in England and the standard in New Zealand, and who seemed delighted in reaching the conclusion that 'we' were every bit as good as 'they'. It is a provincial attitude thankfully on the wane.

I also made a particular point of playing as many balls as possible in the middle of the bat, counting it as a 'black mark' if I edged a ball. I would never try to deflect a ball to third man, only to fine leg. At this stage I think I had a tendency to overestimate the ability of the opposition – there was no rank stubbornness in it – and to under-estimate my own ability. Not uncommon I think, but damaging, and I did desperately want to succeed. This was not batting for the casual spectator, that is up to the established players surely, but runs were going on the board that were useful to me and the side. The inevitable barracking from crowds and the acrimonious attentions of some opposing players made me more determined and forced me to concentrate even harder in order to eliminate outside distractions.

Billy Ibadulla bore the brunt of much criticism at this time, the imputation being that he was responsible for implanting the 'professional' attitude in me. There were no concessions made to the possibility that I might have opinions of my own and the ability to make up my own mind on a few things. My countrymen had (I say 'had' hopefully) such a ridiculously inaccurate idea of what professional cricketers were like, thinking they were all dour, taciturn and parsimonious. One might just as well have said that all New Zealand cricketers were given to fits of pique and temper, were prone to shows of cricketing ignorance and naivety. If you have a cap then someone can be found to wear it. It would be a pity, say, if Trevor Bailey of England and Essex were remembered only for his dogged courage, and his merits as a very fine all-rounder were overlooked, just as it would be sad if the cricketing intelligence and numbers of witty 'characters' in English cricket were overlooked, or if we were to forget the number of eminently sensible and level-headed cricketers playing in New Zealand.

When I began to open the innings I found I was getting out caught in the slips, like many openers, far too often. The reason, which was very simple when I thought about it, was that I was playing at balls I had no need to play. This brought home to me how vital it is to know where your stumps are, and a good way to practise this is to let balls go while practising in the nets even to the extent where sometimes one might knock your off-stump over. I realise this might be hard to take but if you do this you will get to the stage where, when

122

you've been bowled in a game (which I hope won't happen too often), you should be able to nominate, without looking back to see, which stump the ball has hit.

I believe that you reduce your chances of error enormously if you stand as still as you can, leaving any movement towards the ball until the latest possible moment. There are some very good players, Geoff Boycott for example, who move back and across their stumps just as the bowler is about to deliver the ball, but this needs to be a very controlled movement, and is inadvisable for the inexperienced player.

I continually notice many players, mainly because of nervousness and particularly early in their innings, moving about so much that by the time the ball has been delivered, they have absolutely no idea where their stumps are. You must not think of the ball as a hand-grenade coming at you that must be disposed of as quickly as possible. It is only a round piece of leather (hard, admittedly) that has far less chance of hitting you (if this is your main concern) or getting you out if you stand still and allow it to come to you. It is not a boomerang hat is going to stop just short of you and return to the bowler.

I am not suggesting that you relax to the point where you become slow or complacent; keep yourself on edge yet firmly under control. Do not move your feet in response to the first line of flight your eye detects. This is the line your eye picks up just after the ball has left the bowler's hand. If you do this you are committing yourself too soon. By the time the ball has reached you, it may well have moved to the extent that you are struck on the pad because you have gone so far across that you have had to play across the line in an effort to strike the ball, or it has moved away towards the slips, and to play it means playing a long way from your pad. Wait and let the ball do its work before committing yourself to the shot.

A bowler's variation in pace will also confuse a player who commits himself too soon. This fault becomes even more exposed when a slow bowler is bowling. Most batsmen enjoy going down the pitch to a slow bowler whenever they can. So often I have seen a bowler give a delivery a lot more air than usual and lure a batsman down the wicket. The batsman finds himself not getting to the pitch of the ball and is left stranded. If the batsman had only paused he would have detected that the ball had been bowled at a much slower pace, and had he stayed his ground he could have hit it to any corner of the park off the back foot. The impetuous player will never make runs consistently.

In my view, above all else, the positioning of the head is the key to success. It governs the positioning of the feet, balance, poise, timing, and is responsible for judgment of line and length. If one's head were attached to one's left shoulder (right shoulder in a left-handed player), how much easier it would be.

Although there is scope for individuality in most aspects of cricket, there are nevertheless many things which one must get right in order to assist in the elimination of errors. It is so important to begin in the correct position, and so the correct positioning of the head in the stance is vital.

When taking up the stance all effort should be made to keep the eyes level and parallel to the ground with the head tilted slightly forward. A common fault is for the head to be leaning too far over towards the off-side. This is often brought about as a result of the knees being locked instead of slightly bent. When a player is too stiff in the knees, not only is the weight thrown back on to the heels (instead of being on the balls of the feet), but the backside tends to be pushed further out and the trunk is then thrown further across to the off-side in order to maintain any semblance of balance. By bending slightly at the knees and so bringing one's weight slightly forward on to the balls of the feet, the trunk of the body is able to stay more upright. This enables you to get your head into a good position with the eyes level and parallel with the ground, and for you to stand in a good, balanced position.

I believe it is essential for the head to be tilted slightly forward as an aid to balance and, paramountly, as a vital element in the correct transfer of weight when playing forward and back.

When playing forward you can only get the full extension of the front leg and all your weight transferred on to your front knee if your head is tilted forward. If your head is not tilted forward then you will find that it will take much longer to get into the ideal front foot position for up to fifty per cent of your weight will have remained on your back foot. This results in two major problems:

1. the head is further away from the ball and this inhibits judgment of l ne and length and
2. attempts to drive the ball are very likely to result in the ball being lifted.

Even when playing from the back foot one should still keep the body as upright as possible by holding the head slightly tilted forward. If the head is allowed to fall back, then to stay on your feet it is necessary to arch one's back or shuffle back taking a number of unnecessary small steps. When this happens your head is likely to be thrown out of the line of the ball, your timing is usually lost, and once again your judgment of the line and length of the ball is impaired.

Another common fault when playing back to balls pitched outside the off-stump, either when attempting to hit the ball through the covers or simply playing defensively, is for the head and the left shoulder to be thrown out of line. Most players end up with their back foot positioned correctly (i.e. the foot is parallel to the batting crease) after some coaching, but instead of bringing their front foot back in the same line they tend to bring it back too far, dragging it around so that it may even finish up on or outside the leg stump. In other words they square up, become chest-on to the bowler. The likelihood of error in this position is considerable. I advocate that the left leg be withdrawn until it is about twelve inches away from your back leg. This ensures that balance is maintained. Never end up with your feet together.

Those who have difficulty in getting their eyes level and their chin close to the left shoulder in the stance should open their stance up a little so that they become slightly chest-on. But keep this to a minimum as squaring up can lead to many bad habits. Batting is basically a side-on exercise.

I think all batsmen should be very conscious of the importance of keeping the head still at all times throughout every stroke, from beginning to end. The old saying, 'keep your head down', is too often incorrectly interpreted by players who think this means they should dip the head just prior to making contact with the ball. To have the forehead pointing steeply towards the ground is to exaggerate and indulge in unnecessary head movement. Also, at this point, it is difficult to maintain balance. To say, 'watch the ball on to the bat' is a far better and more accurate way of putting it. Move the head as little as you can, just use the eyes to watch the ball, not only on to the bat, but off it as well.

Another misconception occurs when one is told to 'get right over the ball' when playing forward. This quite often results in the leading knee being bent so much, and the bat being angled forward so far, that one's gloves (or hands) are absurdly close to the ground. In this situation the ball can too easily fly from the gloves, whereas it would have been simpler and safer to have stood up more. The ball can still be kept down and the head is in a far better position to judge the line and the bounce of the ball.

Whenever possible it is the wise thing to remain upright during almost every stroke with the odd exception, such as when sweeping. Therefore try not to adopt a crouched stance. Make use of your height.

It is very important to give yourself ample time before the start of a day's play, not only to have a net or a knock-up, but to allow yourself to get prepared mentally.

I always try to arrive at the ground one and a half hours before play starts – have a short net whenever possible, then go back into the pavilion for a cup of tea with half an hour to go. In most cases captains toss up half an hour before the commencement so that you know whether you're batting or fielding in good time. If we are fielding I'll go out on to the ground and have a few short catches – this is because I'm a slip fielder, but if I were an out-fielder I would certainly have some throwing and high catches. However, if I am batting I pad up fairly smartly and certainly allow myself at least ten minutes free time for sitting down and quietly thinking about my innings ahead.

126

For batting I wear quite different clothing from what I wear in the field. I like to use a pair of trousers which have a lot more room in them so that they give me far more freedom of movement. They also make it easier to put in a thigh pad and box. The athletic support is generally a newer one, a lot firmer than those I use for fielding in because it is so important to wear one which will hold a box in securely. I like to wear a light-weight pair of boots as well, a lot lighter than the pair I use in the field. I am a great believer in wearing boots with studs in them and not crepe or gym shoes because I do tend to make positive movements when I am batting so I require my feet to grip. If you wear gym shoes you are likely to slip in them. They are not nearly rigid enough in my view.

A lot of players seem to be a little embarrassed at going out to look at the pitch conditions. They feel that they are giving the impression that they are going out there as authorities and the crowd may have a chuckle and have them on. I think it is very important to have a look at a pitch before you play on it. You should do this before each game. After a while you certainly get a better understanding of the wicket and are better able to predict how it will play. You can go through this process before the crowd turns up because if you are getting to the ground an hour and a half beforehand there are unlikely to be many people about. This is another aspect of the game of which you can learn a lot through experience and one ought to build up one's knowledge and experience through continual observation of wickets in this way.

When I am sitting down ten minutes prior to going out to bat, having had a look at the pitch conditions and having a reasonable idea of how it is going to play, I think of the opposition bowlers. Do they swing the ball much, and if so which way do they generally swing it? At what pace do they bowl, and how is the ball likely to bounce on the pitch?

Having thought about these things you must then firmly fix in your mind the way you are going to go about your innings. It is important, when you are out in the middle, to have control over your actions and movements, and to ensure this you must go out to bat with a policy in mind. If you go out to bat without any policy and full of uncertainty then you find that you start doing things that you really don't want to do and you have lost control over your game.

When I first go out to bat I always say to myself, 'Let the ball come, don't go to meet it', and 'Stand very still and play close to yourself and not away from your body'. This is a way of telling myself to stay alert and to restrain myself that little bit. Here again this helps me not to play at balls that are not going to hit the stumps. I think this approach is best early on against the new ball.

If the opposition has a particularly fast bowler in their side then I restrict my back-lift, and don't take the bat back very far at all for the first few overs. This is particularly important when you meet a bowler who has an unusual action; a good example is the South African Mike Procter who has a very unusual action and is brisk as well. I can remember when I played against him for the first time in a pre-season match. He bowled me because of his unusual action and the fact that that ball came on to me more quickly than I had anticipated. Ever since I have always restricted my back-lift when facing Procter. Irrespective of whether a bowler with an unusual action is quick or not you should certainly give yourself time to get accustomed to it.

I am also very conscious of the need to keep my head in the correct position. I keep telling myself to keep my head very, very still. Another aspect of my technique early in an innings is that I tend to have my top hand further around the back of the handle than is usual. Although this restricts my hitting the ball very hard through the off-side I find that it gives me a lot more control over my bat. A good way to test this yourself is to play a forward defensive shot (with your bat slightly off the ground of course), let go with the bottom hand and test the rigidity of the bat and how much control you have over it, compared with when your hand is right round the front of the bat. As time progresses, and I gain in confidence, I bring my top hand a little further around to give myself more freedom of movement. But my hand is never at any stage very far around the front. At most I get around as far as what the

128

M.C.C. coaching book suggests as the ideal, that is where the line drawn from the 'v' between the thumb and first finger meets the back of the bat half way between the splice and the outer edge.

In the stance, although it is very much a matter of individual preference as to how far you have your feet apart, or whether they should be together, I prefer mine to be about twelve inches apart. My knees are slightly bent so that I am on the balls of my feet but I do tend to have more weight leaning forward on to my front foot. This means that I am more accurately described as a front-foot player than a back-foot player. This does not mean that I am unable to hit off the back foot, but it does mean that to quick bowlers I seldom play back, and tend to stand up and play from the crease line. I personally do not see any benefit in playing back to quick bowlers because, by standing where you are, (although it may be said that you are giving yourself two or three feet less time in which to see the ball) you have very little movement of the head at all. Against slow bowling it is rather different, and I'd use the crease more.

Another aspect which I feel is important about the approach to the early part of an innings is not to talk to anyone until you're reasonably satisfied that you've got most things sorted out, that your judgment is good and that you are striking the ball well. Although you must always look to your concentration, I feel it's helpful to relax between deliveries, *once* you are established. So learn to switch yourself on and off; it is too tiring to try and concentrate for every minute of an innings. Switch on when the bowler is coming up to bowl, then if you feel like a word to the umpire or a fielder do so, or perhaps casually take in and enjoy the surroundings which are often extremely pleasant. One of the pleasures to be had from cricket is to be out in the sun in front of a colourful crowd with, perhaps, trees around the ground.

Earlier on, also, it is vital to get all your technique correct, to give yourself time to be able to judge not only the pace of the wicket, but the pace of the bowler; the bounce and also to give yourself ample time to start moving. One finds early in an innings that it is often very difficult to get moving

129

correctly, so when a half-volley comes along I look to make sure that I get my foot to the pitch of the ball and strike it in the middle of the bat, rather than look to hit it for four. I would be quite happy with perhaps two runs off that delivery. Although it is said by some that a half-volley is a half-volley at anytime, whether it be early in your innings or later on, and that it should always be dispatched for four, I don't believe this at all. You cannot expect too much of any player in the early stages because his judgment is unlikely to be good, so it is unfair to expect a player to risk driving hard at a half-volley outside the off-stump when there is a strong chance of him not quite getting to it and so nicking it into the slips. It can be a little different if you are playing county cricket seven days a week and you find that early in an innings you are moving so well, because you are playing so often, that you are able to dispatch it for four. But I certainly don't believe that a player should look to get after the bowling at this point. When a player is getting a limited amount of cricket, as Plunket Shield players in New Zealand do, I think too much is often asked of him in this respect.

You may say to yourself, 'Well, when do I start looking to score more freely? Is it after a quarter of an hour, half an hour, or an hour?' I don't think that you should judge it in this way. You will find that on some days you will start to move better earlier than others. So it just depends on how you feel, on what the conditions are. Obviously, some conditions are more restricting than others, and you must hope that those watching are astute enough to see this. This is the only way you judge it, according to your own assessment of yourself and the conditions on that particular day; certainly not by the watch. This discussion is meant to relate mostly to the start of your first innings. There are times of course when the situation of the game will dictate different tactics, when you may have to look to get after the bowling straightaway. The points I have been making then should be taken to apply only under normal circumstances where you have time to build an innings.

There are basically two types of players; one is a line player, and the other is a length player. A line player tends to be very conscious of getting in behind the line of the ball and is not too concerned about its length, whereas a length player commits his foot movement to the length of the ball. For instance, if it is up to him he is forward on the drive very quickly, and if it is short he is getting back looking to hit it off the back foot, to hook it or cut it. I believe that in the early stage of an innings it is better to be a line player because you cannot be certain of the bounce of the ball and the pace at which it is going to come off the wicket, so to commit yourself to a cut or a hook can sometimes be disastrous. It is better to get in behind the line and perhaps push it away for one or two, or just defend it. Later, when your judgment is much better, you can expect more of yourself and you are able to get your feet into position for these shots with confidence.

In New Zealand, where you get such a variation in bounce, I think you virtually have to be a line player throughout your innings, that is if you hope to get scores consistently. It does mean that you are restricting yourself somewhat, but to be consistent you have little alternative. In New Zealand a bowler can sometimes land one on his own side of half way with absolutely no guarantee that it will bounce very high at all. So often I have seen players get into a pulling or hooking position to find the ball hasn't bounced above stump height and they have been lbw or even bowled as a result. However, I think that after you have become established under good conditions then you start to become a combination of the two. To be a complete player you have to do this. Even when you have been in for some time and you are starting to move well and judge the line well, I think you should still say to yourself 'Let the ball come' or at least wait and see what particular delivery is being bowled to you.

There is a tendency for most of us to almost will a certain delivery to be bowled to us. If you do this, you will almost unconsciously be getting your feet into position for the type of delivery you *want* bowled to you. If it does not come along, then you can be in all sorts of trouble and you may not be able to take advantage of the delivery that is bowled even if it is a bad one. So you must try and clear your mind each time the bowler comes up to bowl and wait to see what he bowls and not anticipate in any way. Rely on your natural ability to make a split-second decision and hope it is the correct decision at the time.

To play a long innings at any time, particularly in hot countries, is a real test of your powers of concentration and is very tiring physically. If you do start to feel tired you must face up to the fact and try and have a breather by coasting along and restricting your stroke play for a while. Naturally the ideal situation is to be able to play fluently throughout but this is not always possible, particularly if you have run a number of threes and you are puffing and blowing. Sometimes it pays just to go and tap the wicket or perhaps not play an attacking stroke next ball.

If you expect to score heavily and consistently then you must be prepared always to put one hundred per cent effort into it. This is anything but an easy thing to do and I would not for one moment suggest that I can do this. I am sure that there are times when all of us batting in the middle want 50 or 100 or 150 and we want them easily. We don't really want to work hard for them. We are just willing or hoping it will happen. The truth is that in order to make it happen we have got to work hard at it. In the game of cricket one can go out and play in an airy-fairy manner or without much application and concentration and still make some good scores providing one has the natural ability. But to maintain consistency you are going to have to be able to put more into it than that.

There are times though when, no matter how hard you try, you seem to be getting out for low scores. We call this having a 'bad trot', and cricket being the game it is, these things are bound to happen from time to time. Playing cricket day in day out you can get affected by a spate of minor injuries which cause you to turn out at less than peak fitness, or you might be off-colour with a touch of the flu. Somehow one must overcome this and battle on even though it is difficult to give oneself a kick in the backside and say 'Come on; come on, I must score runs, I must do well'.

I have noticed that a great many club cricketers don't give

themselves much of a chance of doing well by often failing to arrive at the ground until ten minutes or a quarter of an hour before the start. They are so busy madly rushing to put their boots and pads and gloves on, and then get out into the middle that they haven't given themselves time to think about what they are going to do. The bowler runs in and bowls, the batsman's still a little flustered with his mind not fully on the game, and before he knows where he is he's back in the pavilion and his day's cricket is virtually over.

It is an often-stated truism that the game of cricket is a great leveller and no matter how good you are, you are going to have your failures. It's not unusual for a player to get 100 one day and nought the next. This is very humbling – maybe this is why cricketers are more often brooding and neurotic than arrogant. I doubt if brashness will make a great player.

Earlier on I wrote in some detail of my ideas on slip fielding, and on the reasons for standing where I do. Perhaps I could make a few further points here about fielding in other positions.

I think the gully, silly-point and short-leg fielders have, almost without exception, no alternative but to watch the bat and not the flight of the ball before it hits the bat. The leg-gully and short-forward leg fieldsmen, in particular, should watch the front of the batsman's leading pad waiting for the bat to appear from behind it. When this happens and the bat is being prodded at the ball there is a strong likelihood of a catch.

If you are fielding in the covers you should watch the movement of the batsman's feet very carefully. Watch for signs of whether he's going to attack or defend. If he's obviously going to attack you should slow down the speed at which you're moving in and be prepared to move quickly sideways in either direction. However, when it is obvious that the batsman is going to defend you should move in more quickly, intent on preventing the short single.

Those stationed on the boundary should always be moving in as the bowler approaches the wicket. Stands and packed terraces often make it difficult to pick up the line of the ball and its flight when hit to you in the air. There's not much you can do about this but watch the ball from the time it leaves

133

the bowler's hand. This will give you a better chance of gauging the flight of the ball off the bat before moving into a catching or fielding position. Concentrate on the ball, try and retain your balance, and drive any consciousness of the crowd (usually awaiting the result with a mixture of apprehension and amusement) out of your mind.

The other thing players must hope for is a captain who uses his head and does not overwork his leading bowlers and top-order batsmen by making them field in positions that require a lot of throwing and running about. These days, when a side is often in the field for the best part of two days, it seems daft to me (unless they are poor catchers of the ball) to ask your opening batsmen and bowlers to field in positions that require a lot of running and throwing.

One feature of cricket that is overdone, especially in Australia and New Zealand, is the propensity to build up some players far too quickly if they show some promise, and conversely to dismiss others too quickly if they don't live up to expectations. Unlike many other games you cannot make snap judgments of a cricketer's ability. A cricketer should only be judged over a long period of time, perhaps three to four seasons. I suppose the Press play a very big part in this sort of thing because if a player recognised as very good scores runs it is not always news, but if a young chap who is in his first or second game gets 100 then he is news and is built up very quickly. Sometimes the very good player is more likely to get a mention if he dips out: dipping out becomes news.

I believe undue pressure is sometimes put on young players in Australia and New Zealand who are apt to be elevated to prospective 'Bradman' class on the strength of a couple of good innings. This has the effect of either putting too much pressure on a player, or giving him an exaggerated idea of his ability and level of development. Either way this is undesirable. In a way this is understandable, of course, because of the limited amount of cricket played in these countries compared to England where a player not only gets a lot more time to prove himself, but also a lot more time to disprove his ability. There are hundreds being scored each day in county cricket so 100 in itself is not such a big thing. I soon became very conscious of the difference in attitude towards success and failure in New Zealand compared to England. When you get 100 in New Zealand people tend to shake you by the hand and make a big fuss about it, while in England they just say 'Well played'. The only time a handshake occurs is when you reach a milestone such as 2,000 runs in the season or having been selected to play for your country. Something on that scale. It is not that the attitude is more blasé in one country than the other, it is more a difference in the goals being strived for.

You would think a cricketer had enough things to worry about without falling prey to superstition, yet there are so many people in the game who are this way. Perhaps they have made runs in a certain shirt or when wearing a certain pair of socks, so they feel impelled to go on wearing them. Sometimes you'll go out to bat with an opener who must walk out on the left or the right side, or another who must take first strike and not second, or vice versa. It's amazing; you could go on forever listing little things that niggle at and worry different people. But I have a rather 'anti' attitude towards these things and if anything I would go out of my way to do the opposite in an effort to try and debunk these superstitions.

One very common bogey is to have a certain score or team total that you dread, that you feel you can't get beyond. One such score in England is 'Nelson'. This is 111, and I know that Shepherd of Gloucestershire is a very good example of a player who dreads being on 111 (i.e. team score – more than individual). He even goes to the extent of jumping before the ball is delivered which is supposed to help him beat the jinx and overcome this obstacle.

I open the innings for Worcestershire with Ron Headley and he always takes first strike. He is the senior player and so has the right to choose what he wants to do. He prefers to take first strike, which is fair enough. Some players who take first strike feel that they are going to get the bowler's 'loosener' and perhaps get off the mark early. If you want to look at it the other way, then by being the non-striker first of all, you are able to

135

soak up the atmosphere of your surroundings before you have to face a ball. For me one cancels out the other and I don't care a damn.

I remember returning to New Zealand in 1969 and making my test debut at Eden Park, Auckland, as Graham Dowling's opening partner. As we walked out on to the ground I said to him, 'Are you going to take first strike, or do you want me to, skipper?' Graham being a very polite sort of fellow said that he didn't mind one way or the other and asked me what I would like to do. I couldn't understand this then for as he was the senior player I felt that he should make the decision. In the end, to be very fair, he said, 'Well, I will take it in the first and you can take it in the second.' He felt that this was the best way to do it. Now, whenever I am going out to bat, whether I am the senior player or not, I always ask the other fellow what he prefers to do because it doesn't worry me at all either way. And if he is undecided then I will generally say that I will take it. There are one or two other players around, however, who have different reasons for wanting to take first strike. One of these is that they want to be known as number one so that they go down on the score card as number one and not two. This for some reason or other is vital to them.

13

Playing Spin Bowling

In England, where wickets are left uncovered, you quite often have to play on very wet pitches which quickly turn into what are known as 'sticky dogs'. When conditions are like this, you have to develop the techniques to combat the different types of bowling you'll meet in order to improve your chances of surviving and succeeding. The one thing to remember is that just because a wicket is in very poor condition it does not give you an excuse to fail. In fact, it should make you determined to try harder. Any runs that you get under poor conditions are so much more valuable than a similar score under good conditions. It is often far more satisfying to get 50 on a bad wicket than 100 on a good one.

When playing an off-spinner on a turning wicket there are two basic techniques. Players are divided on which method they use. The first one is that you play most deliveries with your bat alongside and behind the front line of your pad. This, of course, is when you are defending and not attacking. You play with your bat behind your pad irrespective of the line of the ball, whether it is coming down middle or leg or whether it is breaking back from outside off-stump on to the line of off-stump. Then there is the other technique whereby you try and play everything with your bat to the extent that you are rolling your wrists on the ball all the time. If the ball is coming down the line of middle and leg, perhaps turning down the leg side, instead of playing bat-behind-pad you tend to roll your wrists over the top of the ball and try to play it off the face and down into the leg side. You do the same with the ball breaking back from outside off-stump. I believe that one should try to develop and put into effect both these techniques according to the line of the ball.

137

The alteration to the lbw law whereby a batsman can be given out for padding a ball away outside the off-stump, irrespective of whether he's in line with the stumps or not, has assisted the off-spinner. This means that you must play a shot at a ball turning back from the off, otherwise you are putting yourself in great danger of being given out lbw even though you may be hit outside the line. This delivery is not easy to play, but I believe that when it is pitching outside the off-stump and coming in from there, and it is reasonably well up to you, you should play with your bat behind your pad, letting the ball come past the line of your pad and playing it just a little behind. By doing this you usually effectively cancel out the man positioned in the leg-slip area, and also the man who is fielding at what is commonly known as bat-pad. This is the man who is just in front of square on the leg side, very close in. He is mainly there for the nick on to the pad, which tends to balloon there.

It is also important not to play with the bat held too tightly or rigidly; in fact I think you should play forward with the bat held quite limply. The reason for this is that it is now common practice for a man to be positioned just in front of square on the off-side and he is waiting for the pad-bat shot. This chap fields in a stupid point or stupid square cover position, just a matter of three yards or so from the bat. Sometimes the ball will spin on to the inside of your pad, through on to your bat, and if you are playing stiffly at it, it will carry to this fielder. So it is very important that if the ball does hit the inside of your pad and comes on to your bat that your bat is angled down and is fairly limp so that the ball will not carry to that fielder, but drop very close to you.

If the ball is pitching around about middle and obviously going to go down the leg side or down the line of your leg stump, you can either play bat-behind-pad and keep your wicket intact, or you can try and score from it. You can score off these deliveries by letting the ball come fairly close on to you before leaning right over the top of it, rolling your wrists and playing the ball off the full face of the bat down into the leg side. It is vital that you get right over the top of it and play it off the face, because if you play straight at the line and expose the edge of the bat, an edge will carry in the air around the corner. But by getting over the top of the ball, rolling the wrists and playing it around there, you can quite often pick up a number of runs with relative safety.

I can think of two very well-known players who have the two different techniques that I have mentioned. One is Basil D'Oliveira, who prefers to play bat-behind-pad when defending to an off-spinner. The other is Tom Graveney who always looked to score off them by rolling his wrists and playing it around the corner along the ground. A number of players felt that you had a chance of getting Tom caught at short forward leg on a turning wicket because he would play this shot right from the word go when his judgment probably was not 100 per cent. Certainly once he was established he played it very effectively.

When one seeks to attack an off-spinner on a turning wicket it becomes quite a different game, and I think as much as possible you want to get after him. Obviously, when he first comes on, you want to have a look at him; or if you have just come in to bat, you will be playing yourself in and you will be looking to defend. But once you have sorted these things out you must look to score off him otherwise it can become a stalemate. This is something that is almost trial and error and something that you have to practise yourself in the nets in order to understand what you can and can't do. In general terms, when the ball is pitching on the stumps and perhaps going down leg side or coming on to the pads, then the shot over the top on the leg side is on. But you must be very careful here because the bowler is bound to have at least one man out there in the deep. If he is in the widish mid-on position then you must hit the one drifting on to your pads a lot squarer, more towards mid-wicket or just in front of square. If he has two men out there, then you are taking a fair amount of risk, unless the boundary is quite long and you can chip it over them for a couple of runs, rather than trying to hit it for six. Once you have been able to get him away over the top a few times then the field is usually spread more widely, and several ones and twos can be taken. But to do this you have to be in very good form.

To drive an off-spinner on a turning wicket is much more difficult, especially on the off-side. To do this the ball has to be virtually a full toss: anything other than that is really not on. The spinner may bowl his swinger from close to the wicket and try and angle the ball across you towards a slip if there is one. This delivery may be driven through the off-side, but his orthodox delivery seldom can.

The sweep is quite often playable, but you have to be very careful here too, because if the ball is not only turning but bouncing, there is a great chance of getting a top edge, or of the ball gloving you.

In New Zealand at the present time, the number of fielders you can have on the leg side is restricted to five. Although this does not help the off-spinner very much, particularly under conditions where the ball is turning, he does have the assistance of the recent lbw law change. But here again, in first-class cricket in New Zealand there is complete coverage of wickets, so we rarely have to play on a damp wicket. What we do have are wickets which turn without giving much bounce. It is bounce which makes an off-spinner really dangerous, for if the ball is getting up near the glove region it is very difficult to combat. There is a consensus of opinion which maintains that wherever possible, when facing an off-spinner under these conditions, one should look to play back. I am afraid I am not a great believer in this. I think that if you are able to play forward and smother the spin you should endeavour to do it, particularly if you are playing against the off-spinner who can vary his pace without any obvious change in action. Someone who is very good at this is Ray Illingworth, because he gets right round in his action and has almost an out-swinger's action. Because he gets so much body into his delivery, his change of pace is very subtle and is often not detected until the ball is well on its way. One can get into all sorts of difficulties when caught on the back foot with a flatter delivery which is still pitching on a fullish length. In the main, then, one should be looking to play at least half forward nearly all the time.

140

Against someone like Jackie Birkenshaw, who is much more of a flighty off-spinner in comparison with Ray Illingworth, one plays slightly differently. It is always interesting to play against Leicestershire because there is such a contrast between these bowlers. An off-spinner will often go around the wicket under favourable conditions as he has more chance of an lbw decision. If he does this, though, he is not generally going to get as much turn because of this change in angle. Under these circumstances you must be very careful that you don't play the line of the ball with your pad. The bat-behind-pad technique could well result in your being given out lbw even on the front foot.

Many people feel that the answer to all batting problems is to go and meet the ball, to dance down the wicket after it. Although I don't rule out this cavalier theory completely, I do feel that one should only go down the wicket to a slow bowler if you are absolutely sure of getting there. There is nothing more infuriating than being left high and dry, and virtually being run out rather than stumped if you miss the ball. You will find that a very good spin bowler, if he finds that you are successfully getting down the wicket to him, will flatten out quite considerably and bowl more quickly. This forces you to play from the crease. One must learn to play well from the crease before using the method of going down the wicket.

To play a left-arm orthodox spin bowler under turning conditions is quite different from playing an off-spinner. In recent seasons New Zealand players have had great difficulty in playing people like Derek Underwood who, when he came to New Zealand, found ideal conditions for him. When we met him in England in 1969, in the test matches he bowled on wickets after rain had fallen on them. Because he bowls quite quickly and accurately too, anything the ball does off the wicket is done so quickly that you do not have time to correct yourself half way through the shot. You are fully committed right from the beginning. It was quite different, though, in 1973 when the English seam bowlers bowled New Zealand out. The wickets did not assist spinners and the English spinners did not take a wicket against us. In the one test match Underwood played in he did not have any success at all. In the other two of the three tests played, England used Norman Gifford who is a similar type of bowler to Underwood, apart from being a little slower and using flight a little more than Derek does. Norman had no success either.

With the ball leaving the bat, it is necessary to know where your stumps are in order to know what deliveries you have to play and what deliveries you should let go. On most occasions a left-armer will secure your wicket from a delivery which, if you had thought about it, you would have had no need to play at all. You pushed at it and nicked it to slips or to gully (no doubt he had two or three people catching in this area). The one delivery that you must combat and play correctly is the one pitching round about the off-stump on a good length; one that you shouldn't commit yourself right forward to because it still has a chance to turn on you but on the other hand, one that you can't safely play back to, in case it hurries through on you. This particular delivery is one you must play half forward to, by this I mean only extending the front foot half way, standing up very straight, and watching the ball from there off the wicket. If it turns and lifts then you let it go by, or if you are the type of player who instinctively plays at the ball, be very careful that you don't follow it too wide. By not committing yourself fully to this delivery you are giving yourself a better chance of adjusting your shot if you have to, even if the left-armer is someone who is bowling fairly quickly as Underwood does. I know that when I have been in very good form myself I have actually let balls go that have pitched on the off-stump and have not even played half forward. If you watch the ball closely in the air you can tell if a particular delivery has a lot of spin on it. If it has, then you know that it is going to turn past the off-stump. When you do this, of course, be very certain that it is turning a lot and it is not a quicker one or a seamer that you are letting go which will move in and bowl you.

Generally you are not looking to play a left-armer on the on-side. The only time that you play him there is if you get a full half-volley or full toss. To close the face on a left-arm

142

spinner, when it is turning, often leads to a front-edge back to the bowler, or a skied shot into the covers.

I have seen rather interesting fields set to left-armers under these conditions. I have seen them bowl to only two men on the leg side: one on the sweep on the boundary behind square and another one at a straightish mid-wicket. The other men are at slip, gully, a man in the silly-point position, a shortish cover for the slightly lofted drive, and the rest are saving one. I have personally developed a shot whereby I can score off such bowlers under these conditions. When they bowl just outside off-stump, perhaps going further away, I play what is commonly known as a flat batter. This is just like a cut off the front foot or a square slash. Playing this shot you don't look for the length of the ball so much, that is not so vital. The only thing that you concentrate on is the line. If the ball is short outside the off-stump you stand up a little bit more when you play it. If the ball is further up, you are coming further down on top of it. But always you are looking to hit it along the ground. Because you are swinging the bat so hard, if you do get a fair amount of bat on the ball, it will go very quickly. If it is just wide of the fielder it will go for four. Sometimes a man is put out on the boundary to prevent four for the shot and limit scoring to one, but even then you can play it any-where from square cover to third man. So it is a difficult one to cut off. If you happen to get a top edge, often enough the ball flies so quickly and so high that it defeats the slip and the gully. So it becomes a very good 'percentage' shot under these conditions. I even use it under good conditions to a spin bowler who is trying to restrict your scoring by bowling wider of the off-stump. If the shot can be mastered it is certainly worth while. Although I have got out from it a few times, I have certainly scored many runs in this way, and under bad conditions I think it is worth the risk.

When playing under bad conditions, it is natural that you are going to have a lot of fieldsmen around the bat. You can't afford to let this affect you in any way or encourage you into playing a dangerous shot. I often feel that I have a sound enough technique to stick around and one has to have the confidence in one's ability to do this. Because the fielders are around the bat when you get a bad delivery you have a better chance of putting it away for four. But don't be upset by these crowding tactics.

Two other types of bowler that can be difficult to play are leg-break googly bowlers and the chinaman and googly bowler. They have the advantage of being wrist spinners which means they can sometimes get more work on the ball. They can also impart more over-spin and as a result get more bounce. Because it is so difficult to bowl this type of spin there are very few good spinners of these types around. You are likely to get far more loose deliveries from these bowlers, but if it is their day, and they are landing them on a length consistently, they can be far more difficult to play than the orthodox spinner. To play them well you have to be able to read which way the ball is going to turn or you will find yourself very restricted by them. If you are having difficulty picking it from the bowler's hand, really concentrate on the ball during its flight and see if you can pick up which way it is turning in the air, even though you may not be able to determine this until the ball is half way down the pitch. Unless you pick it up before that, you may not be able to get your feet into position quickly enough to play a scoring shot, but you will certainly be able to defend it satisfactorily. I am sure that a lot of people think that the ball is like a lump of coal coming down at them. But if you really look hard at it, you don't have to have exceptional eyesight at all to see which way it is turning. With all spinners you must try to detect which way the ball is going to turn as soon as possible otherwise your shot-making will be severely limited. Some players seem able to wait until the ball moves off the pitch before deciding on which stroke to play, but not many.

Bishen Bedi is undoubtedly the best left-arm orthodox spinner in the world at the present time and not only is he effective under bad conditions but he also succeeds under good conditions. He has subtle variation of pace like Illingworth and his control of flight and line is impeccable. He has a great temperament as well – this may sound hard to accept by some people, but Bishen loves bowling against players who try to get after him and he is the first to applaud a good shot off his own bowling. He really enjoys playing the game. Mind you, he can afford to applaud a good shot because most times he will end up the winner. I remember when he first came in to bowl to me. It was just as if he was loosening up in the nets, his run up and his delivery stride were so relaxed – and he seems able to go on like that all day. Like most bowlers when it comes to batting, Bishen thinks it's great fun and loves every run he scores. He is always worth a few laughs when he comes out to bat: his appearance in itself is rather unique in that he wears a mini-turban or, as it is correctly named by the Indians, a *patka*. He wears different colours from day to day. I mention Bedi here as he is such a good model for any player to follow. However, in India's tour of England in the summer of 1974, he appeared to have lost some of his rhythm.

When you come to play on hard and fast true pitches the game becomes entirely different. The Australians experience such conditions far more than we do in England or in New Zealand, so you find that the Australians are more often length players than line players. In England and New Zealand we are far less conscious of length and concentrate on getting in behind the line of the ball all the time. Generally when you get on green, grassy wickets the ball tends to move about off the seam. When playing seam bowlers under these conditions, one has to be very conscious of playing close to oneself, of getting so much closer to the pitch of the ball when driving. This is to cancel out movement off the seam. However, just because a wicket is grassy and green it doesn't always mean that the ball will seam about.`If the wicket is firm underneath then it quickens up and the ball is inclined to skid off the green surface.

When facing an in-swing bowler who is getting a lot of swing, you have to be very conscious of the need to let the ball come to you. You almost have to use the bat-behind-pad technique that you use against an off-spinner. It can be fatal to extend the bat forward of the pad to one of these bowlers with the

145

likelihood of exposing the edge of the bat, giving an around-the-corner chance and leaving a gap between bat and pad.

A batsman should be very conscious of which part of the crease a bowler delivers the ball from. You will generally find that most bowlers endeavour to get close to the wicket with their stock delivery, which gives them a far better chance of an lbw. The closer to the stumps you can bowl from the more likely you are to pitch on line and hit the stumps. By bowling wide in the crease, where the angle is so much greater, a good length ball will invariably have to pitch outside the off-stump if it's going to hit the stumps. So the chance of an lbw when the batsman is on the front foot is far less. But for variation, a number of bowlers will go wider in the crease and this can confuse the batsman and cause him to play away from himself or at a ball that is wider than he thought.

An in-swing bowler is far more effective if he can get close to the wicket and get later swing. If he is going wide in the crease, he might get *more* swing than he gets when he is closer to the wicket, but it tends to be all the way, very much like a banana swing which is angling into the batsman's body all the time. If the batsman is playing slightly behind his pad then he has less chance of getting out. The only time an in-swing bowler should bowl from wide out is when he is bowling to a batsman who is lunging with his bat a long way ahead of his pad. I have seen some in-swing bowlers going around the wicket, when getting a lot of movement, in an effort to give themselves more chance of an lbw. Particularly at a fellow who is playing bat-behind-pad. Here, if the ball does pitch on the stumps and hold up sufficiently they have a chance of an lbw. So as a batsman you must play more at the ball under these circumstances and not play the line with your pad. However, I believe that a right-armer going around the wicket has to do so much more with the ball: he has virtually to bowl an off-break to get an lbw.

A left-arm seamer bowling over the wicket, if he gets in fairly close to the stumps, and because his arm is coming over the stumps, has far more chance of getting an lbw decision. Because left-arm seamers are not as common as right-arm ones,

I suppose the difference in the angle of delivery can sometimes be of benefit to them. Once again, as a batsman, you have to be very careful and should know where your off-stump is, so that you are not pushing wide at the ball.

Quick bowlers have a tendency to push their bouncer down the leg side where it becomes far less effective. If you come across a chap who is trying to hook you and is not making a very good job of it, sometimes it is a good idea to go around the wicket and hence give yourself more chance of bowling it down the off-side or over the top of the stumps. Then he either has to get out of the way or play a self-defensive hook at it.

I know that many of the English umpires are very conscious of where the bowler bowls from in the crease when considering lbws. If you get in closer to the wicket you have a head start on anyone who is bowling wide in the crease. This can lead sometimes, though, to running on the wicket, and you have to be very careful that once you have delivered, you take only one stride before running off to the side of the pitch. There are not many right-arm medium pace bowlers who are able to bowl around the wicket and get sufficiently close in without running on to the pitch They generally have to bowl a lot wider in the crease which once again decreases their chances of getting an lbw decision.

Young cricketers of about school-leaving age are usually fairly set in their ways and although they should never stop looking at their bowling techniques, they should be starting to concentrate more on learning by experience, studying how to bowl to different batsmen. One of the basic things is to know how to bowl under various conditions. If you are bowling on a slowish wicket, you should be bowling a fairly full length. Also, work out whether you are bowling against a front foot player or a back foot player. Naturally you bowl a fuller length to a back foot player. Then work out whether he is a line or a length player. I have discussed this earlier, so I need not give you a definition of this.

By just looking at a batsman in his stance you can generally

147

tell where he's going to be strongest. For example, if you see a chap with a very open stance, chest-on towards you, and he has his hands apart and is holding the bat very low down, then the chances are that he is a big leg-side player and a cutter and a hooker for he is virtually in the position to play those shots before you bowl. But because he is holding the bat low down he will not get a full swing of it and this won't assist him in driving. As he is so square-on, if you bowl a half-volley just outside off-stump, he is going to struggle to get right around and get his foot to it in time to play it. Conversely, someone who stands fairly upright, very side-on and holds the bat very high, will strike you straightaway as being more of a driver of the ball and perhaps stronger on the off-side.

Although most of the time you are looking to bowl very tightly to a batsman, there are times when you do come across a very good player, and it is worth a few runs to try and coax him to do something foolish. Often enough this can be achieved by bowling to his strength earlier on. For example, if a very good cover driver wants to commit himself fully to the shot in the first over, good luck to him, because he has a good chance of making an error. So you can bowl for that for a start. But if he gets established, then you will bowl to restrict him or hopefully to any weaknesses you can see. Most of the time you are looking to get a batsman out, but there are times when you have to be prepared to take second place. When the shine has gone from the ball, for example, and the pitch is taking very little turn, and you are playing against a very good batsman who has been batting for some time; then you will have to bowl for a while in a manner to contain and not necessarily looking to get him out. So it is important not only for a batsman to know when to attack and when to defend, but likewise for a bowler. This is the time when the temperament of a player shows. So many quick bowlers, when there is some stick flying around, when conditions don't suit them, really don't want to face up to the fact. That sort of bowler can be compared to a batsman who, when conditions are not very good, can't be bothered battling it out, and who wants to be back in the pavilion waiting for the day when conditions will suit him.

148

Although I only played a couple of times against Fred Trueman, he had the reputation of always wanting to bowl and was a tireless worker. Someone who I know rather better, who is not known as a world cricketer, but whom I have played Plunket Shield cricket with, and who toured Australia with the 1974 New Zealand side, is Brian Andrews. I have never come across anyone else who always wants to bowl, under any circumstances, as much as Brian does. He believes that he has no chance of getting a wicket unless he is bowling, and it is very difficult to take the ball from him because he always wants one more. 'Just give us another one, I think I am going to . . . look just give us another one.' It almost gets to the stage when you feel embarrassed to take the ball from him. We can certainly do with chaps like him in any side.

14

1,000 Runs by the End of May

At the start of the New Zealanders' 1973 tour of England, the prospect of anyone in the New Zealand side scoring 1,000 runs before the end of May couldn't have been further from anyone's mind. For me it did not mean much more than just another tour, another round of the various English counties that I've come to know very well. I naturally wanted to do well, but that is nothing new for me, and it didn't make me differ from the other batsmen in the team. But if my thoughts were far from thinking of 1,000 runs before the end of May the Press, in particular, didn't allow them to stay that way for long.

After three innings on the tour I had scored well in excess of 300 runs, this total including an innings of 143 against my own county, Worcestershire. So, well before I'd reached the 500 mark people, and the Press, were talking of the possibility that I could actually achieve the target that hadn't been reached for more than thirty years – *if* the weather stayed fine, I held my form, had the necessary luck – and so on. At this point, though, I thought it was far too soon to be talking of such a possibility – I know what the weather alone can be like in May, and I know how a batsman's form can fluctuate – and I wasn't confident at all.

It is fairly obvious why the Press so early jumped on to the possibility of my getting the runs. There wasn't all that much going on in the sporting arena at that time, and I'm sure they were also well aware that due to the considerable amount of one-day limited-overs cricket being played these days, the chances of a player performing this 1,000-run feat were becoming less and less.

But when I neared the 800 mark I *had* to concede that it was

151

on and with the Press and now television taking a really big interest in me I felt I had a responsibility to myself and to the members of the New Zealand side to go for the runs. I was close, it seemed to be important to the boys in the New Zealand side, and it was good publicity for us prior to the test matches, so I though it ought to be done. I would like to say here that I don't like chasing records; I have never looked to them, preferring always to take each innings as it comes. If people wish to refer to me as being 'run hungry' then that is all right by me, providing that it is not an allusion to, or another way of imputing, selfishness. I should like to be absolved of that accusation once and for all – the chase for 1,000 runs in May was something that came close to being foisted upon me, not that I have any regrets now at having gone for it.

One thing in my favour early in May was the condition of the pitches. They were mostly dry and fairly true, good wickets to bat on, and this helped me get away to such a good start. A disadvantage, if you can call it that, was that the county sides were nearly all out to get as much practice as they could and so they were all prepared to let their opening bowlers loose. Later on in the season – touring sides who come to England during the second half of the season experience this – the counties are quite likely to rest their opening bowlers when a touring side comes along. This didn't happen to us, obviously.

While the spectators were very interested in my progress right from the early stages, not many of the opposition players showed much interest until the second to last game at Leicester. Until then the players in opposition sides were quite sedate and made little fuss about it all, as is the way in England. I came to Leicester with five playing days remaining in which to score the 133 runs I still required and everything seemed to be ideally prepared for me: the day was fine, the wicket placid. Here was my opportunity to get a big score, perhaps to knock off most of the runs needed. But I batted very badly and made 30 only, and the way I played I was lucky to get that many. In the second innings I was 10 not out when rain completely washed out the last day's play. I thought then that the rain had robbed me of all chance.

We travelled to Northampton with two days remaining in which to score the runs, 93 of them. It seemed a lot to be aiming for, and it was almost certain that I'd have one innings only in which to try to get them. To make matters worse it had been raining in Northampton and the start of the day's play was delayed so that we had only 160 minutes on the first day. Northants put us in to bat, and while some people said they did this in order to give me the chance of scoring the runs I needed, it was not like this at all. The wicket was 'sticky'; Northants weren't being generous. I soon found that out, for at the beginning of the innings it was a dangerous wicket to bat on. The ball was taking off and while I got a share of these I think Bevan Congdon, who was in at at the other end for most of the time, got even more nasty ones than I did. My initial reaction was that if I could get a big score on this wicket then it would give me just about as much satisfaction as the scoring of 1,000 runs. The ball was leaping around so much that I decided that if it continued in this way for much longer, then I was going to give it a flirt – anything I thought I could hit I was going to lay into as I felt I was liable to get out at any stage. So in the first period of play I played fairly freely and actually missed several times when trying to whack it. Then the wicket levelled out somewhat as the hardness went out of the ball. It was at this point that I thought, 'This is a bit foolish.' I felt that if I got out playing a bad shot I'd never forgive myself so I decided to graft and make sure that if I did get out it would more likely be as a result of a nasty delivery than a mistake on my part. The innings I did play differed from most of my innings for, due to conditions, I played the cut and hook quite often, particularly the cut. A perusal of the run chart for this innings will show that. I usually play with the full face of the bat as I like to drive off the front and back foot. It is interesting to compare the run chart for this innings with the one which brought up my tenth hundred of the season for Worcester in 1970.

At stumps I was 70 not out. I'd resisted the temptation to try to

Glenn Turner's 1,000 Runs In May

NEW ZEALAND v. NORTHAMPTONSHIRE 30th, 31st MAY, 1st JUNE 1973
NEW ZEALAND 247–6 decl. TURNER c MUSHTAQ b BEDI 111

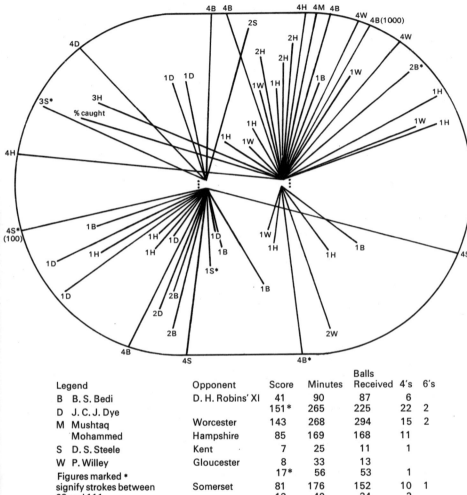

Legend		Opponent	Score	Minutes	Balls Received	4's	6's
B	B. S. Bedi	D. H. Robins' XI	41	90	87	6	
D	J. C. J. Dye		151*	265	225	22	2
M	Mushtaq	Worcester	143	268	294	15	2
	Mohammed	Hampshire	85	169	168	11	
S	D. S. Steele	Kent	7	25	11	1	
W	P. Willey	Gloucester	8	33	13		
Figures marked *			17*	56	53	1	
signify strokes between		Somerset	81	176	152	10	1
93 and 111			13	49	34	2	
Compiled by I. M. Walter		Glamorgan	53	108	105	9	
			44	62	69	3	
		M.C.C.	153*	315	285	16	1
TOTAL			3	6	6		
11 matches, 18 innings,		Derbyshire	2	11	7		
5 not outs, 1018 runs,			66*	98	83	7	1
153 not out highest		Leicester	30	113	107	2	
score, 78.30 average.			10*	43	32	1	
Scored in 35 hours 42		Northampton	111	255	247	15	
minutes, from 1978 balls							

knock off the runs that night, deciding to hang on and wait for the next day. The rest is history. I did feel greatly relieved when it was all over and it did give me considerable pleasure and satisfaction to have achieved the goal. I felt as pleased for the side as I did for myself; I think the publicity did us a lot of good.

Many people have remarked to me about my apparent lack of emotion on and off the cricket field. I am certainly no cold fish, and I feel very strongly and passionately about some things. But when I was younger I was convinced that if I showed too much emotion then this was likely to result in the rash moments which lead to the making of mistakes. I have never had much respect for the player who tosses in the sponge without putting up a fight. Nowadays I have a much more carefree attitude to the game: I look to get on with it more, my game is centred on attack more than defence; in other words I am giving the bowlers more of a chance. Perhaps I am no longer as disciplined as I should be.

The pressures off the field were in some ways as difficult to deal with as those on it. The Press and television focused on me, naturally, and I found it hard to cope with two interviews in particular which took place just before I was due to go out to bat. I didn't really like going through these even though I appreciate the need for, and importance of, sportsmen making themselves available to the media as much as possible. There must be give and take here, and as long as journalists and interviewers realise this then there need be no trouble or allegations of aloofness. Experienced newsmen appreciate this I think, and should they have their differences with a sportsman they should try to have it out with him and clear the air as soon as they can. I also had phone calls from newsmen at night – what about a man's social life?

After the event I was swamped with letters and telegrams, ar more than I could hope to answer. I'm not a good letter writer anyway; I struggle to communicate with my friends even in this way. With the help of Dick Brittenden I selected a few here and there for reply, especially those from New Zealand schools. I was delighted to receive so many letters of congratulation and thank everyone for them.

How was the 'clock-work machine' going to function in the tests against England? We all know the answer to that now: no damn good! I hadn't been reading what the critics were writing, but one or two English friends said to me that I would have to be very careful that I didn't do what someone before me had done after scoring the coveted 1,000 in May, and that was to have a very poor test series. So I was wary, perhaps too wary, I don't know. The build up of pressure before the end of May must have had some effect though, because when it came to the tests I went through the usual set of questions I ask myself – Who are their bowlers? What do they bowl? What are the conditions like? and so on. From the answers to these questions I work out a list of do's and don'ts. For example, if you're going to face a bowler like Geoff Arnold who's an out-swing bowler you say, 'Right, anything just outside the off stump I'm not going to play at' – so that's a don't. Or with John Snow, who's sharpish, you say, 'I'm not going to hook him' – that's a don't. But I found myself doing these don'ts and not having much control over my actions and this was something new for me. Perhaps it is true when people say that on a tour you should use the games prior to a test series simply to build up form for the series, but in my case I had built up to a peak at the end of May and I felt flat. Mentally I was not in the right state of mind.

I don't want to take anything away from the English opening bowlers; their bowling early on was excellent. Conditions were of assistance to them, it was a bit humid and there was some 'juice' in the wicket. Snow and Arnold are fine bowlers. I do believe, though, that you must always back yourself, no matter what the conditions, and blame yourself for your mistakes and try not to admit that the other chap was too good. Blaming other people doesn't breed success. I largely got myself out.

Some of the other New Zealand batsmen played well, especially Bevan Congdon and Victor Pollard. John Parker and I did not, but while we scored few runs we more than once batted for up to an hour, so both the quick bowlers had bowled six or seven overs apiece. This time element was important

156

HODDER AND STOUGHTON LIMITED

SAINT PAUL'S HOUSE WARWICK LANE
LONDON EC4P 4AH

REVIEW COPY

MY WAY
Glen Turner

To be published on
19 May, 1975
at £3.25

to those who followed. All the time we were fortunate, of course, in that whenever Bevan came in to face the music he nearly always saw it through and in this series we saw some very fine batting from him. Vic usually came in when most of the terrors weren't there any longer, though his results show he played well irrespective. Mark Burgess also played a couple of splendid innings.

The English spinners didn't take a wicket in the series so the English side was aware of how vital it was to chip us out when the ball was new. The pity of our unsuccessful opening stands in this series was that we were unable to bat longer than we did – the number of runs we scored were of secondary import-ance. If we'd stayed around longer then it would have been easier for the batsmen to follow. I think cricket observers generally tend to underestimate the importance of the time taken up by an opening stand, as opposed to the number of runs scored. Many people seem to feel that a good start can only be judged by the number of runs on the board, and by how quickly they are put there. They say that it can have a depressing effect on the batsmen to follow if runs don't come up quickly. We all agree that the ideal is to have runs coming in freely from the outset while no wickets are being lost, but in a five-day match the openers' first responsibility is to see the shine off the ball and the opening bowlers off. *That* has a depressing effect on the fielding side, if you are given to fits of psychoanalysis. It must surely be expected that experienced players batting down the order are mature and sensible enough not to allow what is happening, or has happened above them, to dominate their thinking and influence the way they are going to play.

I was not pleased at my lack of success in the series against England and my feelings when it was over were a mixture of annoyance and perplexity and disappointment. The New Zealand side returned to New Zealand and I went back to Worcester, where I managed to make over 1,000 more runs in what remained of the season. At times I played as well as I have ever played, or better.

I have been asked if I would like to bat at number four, say,

157

in the order. In some ways I would, as I think I might find it a little easier, but if one wants to make really big tallies in a season then opening is the position to do it from. This particularly applies to three-day cricket. With test cricket it would be different, but to drop oneself down the order would be a selfish attitude. Someone has to face the music, so to speak, and it is best that your better players do it.

If the opportunity presented itself again would I try for 1,000 runs before the end of May? It's unlikely that I could ever string those scores together again, but if the possibility loomed again I would try for it. I don't believe that it would necessarily affect my results in a future test series; I wouldn't allow myself to be 'affected' by past experience. That would be a weak and cowardly thing to do.

15

Victory over Australia, 1974

New Zealand toured Australia during the 1973–74 season and for the first time were accorded the privilege of a test series against a fully-fledged Australian side. From a personal point of view I had an unhappy tour and only in Tasmania, where I've done well before, did I really get going. I broke a bone in my hand in the third match of the tour, against New South Wales, and this was to trouble me for the rest of the tour.

I was fielding at first slip when one of the New South Wales openers, Ron Crippen, went to cut a ball from Richard Hadlee. It flew off the top edge and grew big on me, coming straight at my head. I had to move my head quickly to one side so my hands moved out of line with my head and I consequently misjudged the line of flight. As soon as the ball hit me I knew that a bone had been broken and I left the field immediately and went off to have it X-rayed and put in plaster.

Everyone was anxious for me to play in the first test at Melbourne which was to start three weeks later, especially since we had gone to Australia with a somewhat less than full strength side; at least three of our better players, Hedley Howarth, Mark Burgess and Richard Collinge having been unavailable to tour.

This anxiety that I should play resulted in my making the mistake of consenting to play at Melbourne before I felt that my hand was properly mended. As it happened I might as well not have turned out for soon after the start of our first innings I was hit on my injured hand and batted on for a while in some pain, out of stubbornness, until I was dismissed for a mere six runs. I took no further part in this match and had to miss the second test in Sydney.

The second test was a match we seemed poised to win until rain washed out the last day's play, so instead of going to Adelaide for the third test with the series level 1-all, we were one down. By this stage of the tour I must confess I was on what the Americans call a 'down'. I was almost uninterested in the cricket, and was experiencing serious problems of mental motivation.

In our first innings I cruised sedately to 20, feeling comfortable and in control, until the tea-break arrived. The wicket was true, but on the slow side. In many ways it was a docile wicket. 'You can't get out on this wicket,' I said, 'unless you do something stupid.'

I came out after tea and prepared to face the first ball from Hurst. Just as he started his run up a friendly seagull left its mark on me. I pulled away and effected some running repairs saying to a couple of the nearest Australians, 'It must be good luck'. Well, it wasn't. Hurst bowled me a straight one and for some unknown reason I fell towards the off-side as he released the ball which hit me on the pads. 'Oh, oh,' I said, 'that could be close.' It was too close. It was out.

In the second innings I got to 34, again comfortably, before I played a little loosely when trying to hit the ball forward of point and Kerry O'Keefe took a good catch in the gully.

We were soundly beaten in this match and returned to New Zealand having lost the series 2–0. We all felt that it would perhaps have been a fairer result if the series had ended 1–2, even though we hadn't played consistently well at any time on the tour.

Returning to New Zealand we found most cricket enthusiasts eagerly awaiting the arrival of the Australians for the return series. We felt that under our own conditions, and with all our leading players, with the exception of Mark Burgess, available for the entire series, we would give a much better account of ourselves.

The New Zealand team assembled in Wellington a few days before the first test intent upon at least two full net practices before the match began. Our first practice was held at the

lenn plays his "slash"

balance and concentration

Basin Reserve where conditions were adequate, but the next day, the day before the match, we were shifted to the Kilbirnie ground and the practice strip was not up to standard. Presumably the recent weather was partly responsible for the strip was far too soft and was dangerous for all but the few who batted first. So we were to go into the first test knowing that our pre-match preparation wasn't really adequate.

In recent seasons the Basin Reserve has acquired the reputation of having the quickest, bounciest and truest wicket in New Zealand – this wasn't always so by any means. When we went to look at it on the day before the match we found it wasn't as heavily grassed as we'd expected, and there seemed to be no real depth of hardness in it. (As we were to find out each of the wickets we were to play on in the series had surprises in store for us – they were atypical rather than typical.) A look at the roller that was being used made it fairly obvious why the wicket wasn't hard: it was quite light, of the type you sit on and drive up and down on while the wicket is being cut at the same time. We realised then that the wicket would have little pace in it, that there would perhaps be some slight movement off the wicket, but that was all.

The New Zealand squad for the test included four medium to medium fast bowlers: Richard Hadlee, Dayle Hadlee, Richard Collinge and Murray Webb, and the decision as to which of them was to be twelfth man was not going to be easy to make. Murray had taken forty wickets in the recent Plunket Shield series and had bowled an average of nearly twenty overs an innings; Richard Collinge had regularly performed well for New Zealand and would have the added incentive of playing on his home ground; Dayle had done well on the recent Australian tour and his brother Richard had also performed adequately there. None of them really deserved to be left out.

One possibility initially was that a medium pacer, someone like Lance Cairns, could have been brought into the squad, for in a five-day match at the Basin Reserve you can expect the wind to blow quite strongly on at least three of the five days. As the wind nearly always blows straight down the wicket, either from the north or the south, someone has to become the donkey and bowl into the draught. Bevan Congdon was obviously going to have to do some of it, but who was going to open the bowling into it? Another awkward decision to have to make. If the wicket had looked as if it were going to be at all lively then we would have given consideration to playing all four quick bowlers, yet this would have meant dropping a batsman, something we didn't want to do, and batting Ken Wadsworth at number six. While Ken got runs in Australia we felt that number seven was his rightful place, in spite of suggestions to the contrary from some people in New Zealand and in Australia. Ken always plays better when the shine is off the ball and the sting has gone out of the quick bowlers. He is a good player of medium pacers. The other point against Jlaying all four quick bowlers was that we didn't want to drop peremy Coney. In the end Richard Hadlee drew the bad marble.

It rained a lot on the night before the match and water seeped under the covers at one end and there was a damp strip on the wicket just on or outside the right-hander's leg stump. I must say, and I say it without malice, that the covers at the Basin are or, I hope, were, rather antique. It is always the old story, 'New covers are on the way and will be ready for any future series'.

This wet patch was going to be of use only to a right-armer bowling round the wicket or a left-armer bowling over the wicket. The score was even here: they had the left-armer Geoff Dymock and we had Richard Collinge.

We didn't have to concern ourselves over whether to bat or not for, as anticipated, the Australians won the toss and decided to bat first. Unfortunately the ball didn't do much off the wet patch, or we didn't land the ball there often enough to find out. Keith Stackpole, who was to have a wretched series, was out with the total at 13, bowled by Murray Webb, and Ian Redpath departed at 55. After this, though, Ian Chappell and his brother Greg gave our attack a pasting in a partnership of 264 runs for the third wicket. The wicket played so easily; the wind blew so strongly. It was certainly no

162

day to be in the field. Greg Chappell, in particular, played some fine strokes and we all put on a fairly good display in the field, chasing the ball around like a team of keen first eleven boys, though always taking care to avoid, where possible, getting our whites dirty. The crowd seemed to appreciate the batting of the Australians who scored throughout at the rate of about 5 runs an over, a very good rate for a test match and an indication of how good the wicket was for batting. Those spectators who might perhaps have been concerned at the Australians' rate of scoring seemed quite happy, lucky people, to take solace in a roseate glow, the cause of which is dispensed in the north-western corner of the ground.

By lunch on the second day the score stood at 511 for 5 and in the first over after lunch Rod Marsh was dismissed and to everyone's surprise Ian Chappell declared leaving Greg not out at 247. This was a fine innings from him, but fortunately for us he never got going like this again in the final two matches of the series.

We went to the wicket aware that we had an awful lot of work to do. I was still concerned about my mental condition; I knew I wasn't mentally as sharp and as keyed up about playing against the Australians as I felt I ought to be if I was to do well. Over the last season, ever since the West Indies tour in fact, I'd been fighting to re-establish a 'hard' attitude and to shed a mixture of sourness and frivolity. I had managed to hide the sourness, if that is quite the right word, but not the light-heartedness or frivolity that was beginning to creep into my batting. Another factor that bothered me was that since our return from Australia I'd batted twice only, once in a club match in Dunedin when I scored 3, and once in a charity match when I scored 7. Something told me this wasn't an intensive lead-in to a test series.

One thing, though, that happened the night before the match made me keener than I might have been to do well. Garry Ward asked me to be his guest, along with the N.Z.B.C.'s number one cricket commentator, Alan Richards, on 2ZB's Sports Talkback programme. I ducked a few questions, answered a few, and then a caller rang in and told me that although

163

he didn't subscribe to the opinion, he knew of a lot of cricketers and supporters who felt that I might be able to do all right in provincial and county matches but I wasn't any good in tests, and he wanted to know what I had to say about that. I wasn't much surprised by what he'd said but I was stung and a trifle annoyed by what I viewed as a mixture of prejudice and ignorance. I didn't say it at the time, Alan Richards said it for me, but I did have a test average of 45 which was something anyone who could be bothered to read the statistics could find out. All I did say in reply was to admit that I had had a poor series in England the season before, after I'd scored 1,000 runs by the end of May, and that I thought that the game of cricket was not a game in which a player's ability should be judged over a short period of time. I was also told the story, while in Wellington, of how, while on the 1973 tour of England, one of the local lads had bet the sports editor of one of the Wellington papers that I wouldn't total 100 for the series. It just shows you that it's not always only the opposition bowlers who are trying to get you out. The amusing side of it was that that chap was nearly right, but not quite. I'm glad he lost his bet.

We started quite well and even though we lost John Parker with the score at 28, John Morrison and I took the score through to 136 before I was out, caught low down by Ian Redpath at cover point for 79. I was reasonably satisfied with this score though I felt I should have got a century. Kerry O'Keefe bowled me a ball of fairly full length which was perhaps a little too wide for the shot I tried to play. I tried to drive it through the covers for four but didn't quite get to the pitch of the ball. In retrospect I think it must have stopped a little on pitching, rather than turned, or I'd have edged the ball towards slip or gully.

After John Morrison departed early next morning when the score was 169, Bevan Congdon and Brian Hastings put on 229 for the fourth wicket to take us through to the comparative safety of 398 for 4. Both Bevan and Brian scored centuries but after they got out we folded to be all out for 484.

We had taken eleven hours fifty minutes for our innings at a run rate well below that of the Australians, our rate being under 3 per over. In many ways this was to be expected for when you are chasing such a big score as theirs you are not going to be able to win the game, so even if it takes you some time it is vital to get a big total and this is what we succeeded in doing.

The Australians went in for their second innings and at stumps on the fourth day were 86 for one wicket. They then batted for the whole of the fifth and final day to be 460 for 8 wickets at the close, Ian Chappell and Greg Chappell again making centuries. Conditions for the match were miserable, a cold, strong wind blowing nearly all the time. I think Chappell's decision not to declare on the fifth day could be defended. We had batted for a long time, for nearly twelve of the thirty hours of the match, and his bowlers had bowled forty overs or more each. He obviously felt there wasn't going to be sufficient time to bowl us out even if he did declare. I suppose he thought that to declare would be merely to make a token gesture, and that seeing the second test was to commence in Christchurch with only one day in between, he felt his chaps would be better off sitting in the warmth while we toiled away in the cold. Nevertheless, I'm inclined to feel that you are obliged to make some sort of declaration, for everyone knows that strange things can happen in cricket, even if he'd set us a stiff task. Maybe if things had gone his way and we'd got into trouble, who knows what might have happened. But either argument has its points for and against, and we couldn't really quibble about his decision.

After spending the best part of two very cold days in the field in Wellington we didn't want to have a tough practice when we arrived in Christchurch the next day, but most of our batsmen did want another knock in the nets before the second test. I certainly did because I'd had one innings only in Wellington and that was my first for sometime. We arrived in Christchurch to find that they had had a lot of rain there and that the only net available at Lancaster Park had been given to the Australians. All we could do then at the Park was run around and have a bit of fielding practice. This was unsatisfactory and a trifle annoying.

165

Naturally we were keen to have a look at the pitch and I was quite astonished at the amount of grass there was on it. I had played there before Christmas in a one-day match prior to our departure for Australia. On that occasion the wicket was unevenly grassed, and tufty – in fact it was striped in zebra-like fashion. In between the tufts there seemed to be no binding at all, no depth of hardness to the wicket; and each time the ball pitched it was going through the top and sometimes stopping very noticeably. The wicket's recovery then had been remarkable. The groundsman must have put in a considerable amount of work and he deserves much credit for this. The grass had come through evenly but it seemed that there was just too much moisture in the wicket. We couldn't see how it was going to dry and harden up before the match started. It seemed that if we won the toss we would have no alternative but to ask them to bat.

Rain prevented play on the first morning of the match and we didn't start until around 2.00 p.m. Murray Webb had injured a leg in the test at Wellington so Richard Hadlee returned to the side. Due to the conditions there was no opportunity for us to have a knock-up before play commenced so we were all going to start cold so to speak.

Bevan Congdon quite often before a match calls on the senior members of the side to state their opinion on whether we should put the opposition in to bat or not. I think that this is a wise approach and irrespective of the state of the wicket he usually asks me what I think, even if he doesn't ask anyone else. On this occasion there wasn't really much time to talk about what decision would be wisest, and as he was going out to toss I light-heartedly said to him, 'You don't need to worry anyway because you couldn't win a toss if you tried' – but he did! There was panic stations because with only a quarter of an hour to go before the start we were going to have to make up our minds quickly. Seeing that Brian Hastings was a local and had played a lot of his cricket on Lancaster Park, we called him into our discussion. Neither Brian nor I had seen a Lancaster Park wicket as grassy as this one was, but seeing there was so much grass on it we felt it must do something.

It seemed to be mainly a matter of asking, 'Will it remain green right throughout and so not make a great deal of difference which side bats first?' I confess I was undecided on what was the right decision to make and for this reason I would probably have batted. Brian's vote went for putting them in. As it turned out the scores in the match were between 200 and 250 in each innings so it probably didn't make a lot of difference which side batted first. Psychologically though it seems to have been a good decision and proof of the pudding was in the result.

The Australians lost Stackpole when the total was 4 and then at 45 Richard Hadlee held one back and bowled Ian Chappell. Richard's slower delivery is so much slower than his stock ball that most batsmen have no difficulty detecting it, but on this occasion Chappell tried to hook it away off the front foot, played far too soon and was bowled.

At this point Bevan Congdon, or 'golden arm' as we call him, came on to bowl. Bevan is one of these chaps whose bowling looks innocuous from the side, but who has this habit of 'coming off', and in recent seasons he's done some very good work as a part-time bowler. He bowled to Greg Chappell who slashed at a ball outside the off-stump and it flew off the edge. Hedley Howarth shot a hand high above his head and the ball went smack, straight into it. I was at cover and got as big a surprise as anyone for I was looking for the ball towards the vacant third-man boundary.

My hand, injured in Australia, was still bothering me and I didn't have the confidence to field in my usual first slip position, so for the whole of the series I fielded in the covers mainly, but sometimes at mid-off, mid-on or mid-wicket. I was no stranger to the cover position as I'd begun my first-class career in Otago running around in that position, and in one-day cricket in England one spends quite a lot of time chasing the ball round the paddock.

At the close the Australians had struggled to reach 128 for 5 wickets, with Ian Redpath being not out 55. Redpath hadn't looked comfortable at any stage and he was fortunate to have survived for he'd played and missed time and again. In spite of this he was going to be our biggest threat on the second

167

day and we thought that if we could claim his wicket early then our chances of getting the Australians out for a comparatively low score would be good.

We finally got Redpath's wicket when the score had reached 181. Soon after this we captured the further valuable wicket of Rod Marsh who'd virtually slogged his way to 38 although his innings was interspersed with some good strokes. He lost his wicket in rather an undignified fashion when he went down on one knee and with his head in the air tried to sweep Bevan Congdon. We had Bevan on about this, saying that batsmen normally only attempted to sweep spinners and that maybe Marsh was putting him into that category. Bevan ended up with the best figures among our bowlers of 3 for 33 and the Australians were all out for 223.

We opened our innings a few minutes before lunch and managed to keep our wickets intact until the interval. After lunch John Parker was first to go with the score at 59, but then we lost three wickets quite quickly to find ourselves in serious trouble.

The ball always seemed to be doing something off the wicket, and at no time during the match did it allow you to play with any real freedom. You couldn't afford to risk hitting the ball on the up, for example, so you had to play close to yourself. As long as the bowlers didn't bowl loosely and kept the ball up to you the business of scoring runs was going to be difficult and time-consuming.

At one stage, later in the afternoon, it looked as if I might get to 100 before stumps. I had dallied in the seventies but came with something of a rush in the twenty minutes before the close. With an over and a half to go I was on 99 and facing the bowling. Ian Chappell brought his field in, intent on denying me the single I wanted. It was here that some people got the impression that I'd succumbed to an attack of the 'nervous nineties'. As it happened I wasn't too concerned, but seeing I was on the brink I thought it would be a good thing for us if I could bring up my century that night. Whenever you do approach a century your partner, in this case Ken Wadsworth, begins to back up further than usual so that every time you hit the ball you tend to take off down the wicket and wait for him to give you the 'Yes' or 'No'. Several times I went perhaps three yards down the wicket, rather like a jack-in-the-box, in and out of my crease, but I (unlike some spectators) never felt in real danger of running myself out. The last ball of the day was short outside the off-stump from Geoff Dymock and I cut it right in the middle and hard but straight to point.

No one can say they are used to sitting on 99 overnight, especially in a test match, but it had happened to me before in Dacca in 1969 during a test against Pakistan. We were 194 for 5 on that occasion and I did manage to get my century the next day.

The crowd at Lancaster Park are as responsive as any crowd I've ever played in front of. Their involvement in the play, and their support for the home side is, if a little partisan at times, tremendously encouraging.

Under the conditions it seemed vital that we get a good lead on the first innings and I was keenly aware that New Zealand's hopes of gaining this lead were largely with me. I went to bed then with two unusually pressing responsibilities on my shoulders.

For the whole of the match so far the atmosphere had been damp so the wicket was not drying out at all. The ball was still seaming off the wicket, lifting pieces of green whenever it pitched on the seam.

Ian Redpath had played and missed often enough in his innings of 71 but I had missed even more, particularly in the early stages of my innings. It was almost embarrassing me but I said, 'Dammit, I must fight through it, and even if it takes me all day I'll keep going and see if I can come right.' Towards the end of the day I did hit a few in the middle which scooted to the boundary to make a welcome change for me.

By this stage it seemed as if the whole of Christchurch had its eye turned on the match; the whole town was alive and buzzing with an interest unprecedented in a cricket match. All through the afternoon of the second day the enthusiasm and the tension in the crowd seemed to grow apace with my progress towards my century. The crowd support for me and the

169

rest of the New Zealand side during the match was over-whelmingly encouraging. The tension over the last half hour of the second day's play became almost unbearable.

The next morning I batted for nearly half an hour before scoring the run I needed to reach 100. I was feeling comfortable and hitting the ball in the middle of the bat; some of the shots I played would have gained me several runs under normal circumstances, but because of the situation Chappell had his field set defensively. Then I got out. I played slightly away from myself to a ball from Greg Chappell that lifted consider-ably but was short enough to have left alone and the ball went low to the right-hand side of Stackpole at second slip and I was on my way for 101.

Though I am always philosophical about this sort of thing I left the field feeling annoyed and a little despondent for I felt the side needed more from me. After my departure we didn't have much fight left and our innings closed for 255, a lead of only 32. So once again it seemed that we had failed to ram home an advantage.

There were close on 15,000 people at Lancaster Park (one of the largest crowds they've ever had for a cricket match at that ground) for the third day which was a Sunday. The crowd again seemed keyed-up and excitedly soaked up everything that took place on the field. The acoustics of the stadium are such that crowd noise carries unusually loudly to the players on the field, as some of the Australian players discovered to their displeasure, and we to our concern. The spectators in the Numbers One, Two and Three stands in particular respond magnificently to events on the field and seem very close to the players, or that's the impression they give. As a player, you can feel inspired or threatened; but you are *always* aware of their presence.

The Australians came out to bat for the second time and, as seemed inevitable by now, Keith Stackpole was back in the pavilion early with the score at 16. Then the arrival of Ian Chappell heralded the commencement of one of the most ex-citing and elating periods of play I've ever experienced. It wasn't long before Ian Chappell, for some unknown reason, walked inside a ball from Richard Collinge and was bowled. Ian has a tendency to walk back and across as, or before, the ball is bowled. I think that any player who indulges in this sort of preliminary movement is not always certain where his stumps are and you naturally have your best chance of taking his wicket early in his innings before he has time to pick up the line. It wasn't as if this ball from Collinge did anything unusual in the air (so my spies behind the wicket tell me); Ian simply walked inside the line and so far across in front of his stumps that he couldn't play the ball. I was in the covers and the whole episode appeared to me to be happening in slow motion. Chappell walked across in front of his stumps and then I saw the ball striking his leg stump and the stump bending slowly backwards. I couldn't believe it. Then the crowd erupted and the roar was deafening. For the first time in a long while I felt the shivers run down my spine. I must admit that at this point I got taken up by the atmosphere; my senses had been really sharpened by the crowd that was simmering with excitement behind me and I think most of the other New Zealand players felt much the same way.

Not long after, Richard Hadlee came running in to bowl to Greg Chappell and again it seemed to me that everything was taking place in slow motion, as if there were a long time lag between events. Richard pitched one fairly short and Greg went on to the back foot and tried to crash it past cover for four. As he went to play the shot Richard sensed that it wasn't really 'on' and he started to appeal virtually as Greg was half way through the shot. Then you heard the nick and the crowd erupted again with a great roar; they were so absorbed by the play it was almost as if they were in a state of wilful hypnosis. But the peculiar thing was that the ball had not yet been caught, it was still on its way to Jerry Coney at first slip, although as far as the crowd was concerned it was a foregone conclusion that Greg Chappell was out. It really was a tremendously memorable dismissal and the Australians were 33 for 3. We had made a crippling inroad into their batting even though they still had some strong batting to come.

I think we were fortunate to get Greg Chappell in early

while the ball was still quite new for although he is a very fine player he does like to play freely from the outset, to play nearly all his shots from the word go. On this occasion he attempted what is a very good cricket shot, a shot that is difficult to play and one that most players wouldn't normally attempt until a little later in their innings.

Ian Redpath and Ian Davis held us up and put on 106 for the fourth wicket before Richard Hadlee broke through and took both of their wickets in his eleventh over. Redpath had been playing much better in this innings than he had in his first; his dismissal, though it wasn't controversial for he was clearly out, was unusual and unfortunate for Redpath. When Richard Hadlee lets a bad delivery go he has a habit of grunting in frustration, making a noise as if someone's hit him in the solar plexus. This is what happened here. Redpath heard this noise and mistook it for a no-ball call and cut the ball straight to Hedley Howarth in the gully. He stood at the wicket but unfortunately for him the umpire had no alternative but to give him out as he hadn't called. I was puzzled because umpire Hastie always calls particularly loudly and I'd heard no call from him, but our boys in the slips later conceded that they too had been fooled, as poor Redpath had been, and had thought they'd heard a no-ball call. Immediately after this Ian Davis pulled a ball straight into the hands of Bevan Congdon at mid-wicket, then just before stumps Dayle Hadlee bowled a rank full 'bunger' to Rod Marsh who couldn't resist it and hit it very hard straight back down the wicket. Dayle leapt high to his right and with his arm fully extended found the ball had stuck in his right hand.

We were not all that happy with the stumps score of 211 for 6 as Doug Walters, who'd come in at the fall of Davis's wicket, had very smartly got to 52 not out. He was obviously going to be the big danger on the fourth day and we knew that if we didn't get him early we'd be chasing a total of well over 300 runs. On a wicket still grassy, still green with a lot of moisture in it, this would be a hard target to reach.

The Australians reached 232 before one kept low on Walters and he was trapped lbw to Dayle Hadlee. In fact Dayle captured the wickets of Walters, Walker and Dymock in fourteen deliveries. The last pair put on 20 or more to take the Australian total to 259 before they were all out. This meant that we had to score 228 to win and we had all the time in the world to do this.

I don't think any one of us in the New Zealand side was under any illusions about the magnitude of the task facing us. In some circumstances 228 is not a very big score and we knew that although the pitch wasn't playing all that badly, and that perhaps we really ought to get the runs, we'd always in the past just fallen short of targets or not made full use of the opportunities that we had created. A win to New Zealand was by no means certain and the Australians were particularly keen to see that we didn't get this win.

The atmosphere when we went out to bat was still highly charged. The Aussies seemed, even for them, especially keen and on edge to the extent where, if a bowler bowled anything like a reasonable over, he was encouraged by several of his team mates who kept saying things like, 'Well bowled Tangles (Max Walker)' or whoever it was. Keith Stackpole is very keen on boosting his team mates like this. And even Ian Redpath who is normally a friendly, though unassuming, and basically quiet fellow on the field, was egging his players on too. This of course is a good thing. I even heard Doug Walters open his mouth once in praise. Normally you just don't hear Walters, though you know he's always present, ready to pounce, fielding magnificently. Generally, though, he never says boo on the field. The overall tenseness surrounding the game on and off the field was as great as any I had experienced before, as great as when I had first played for Worcestershire against Yorkshire in 1968.

John Parker and I made another reasonably good start and batted safely until John went with the score at 51. Then John Morrison got out 4 runs later padding off, not offering a shot to Max Walker. I sympathise with John for it is not easy to come in and face someone like Max Walker, because he moves the ball appreciably in the air and once it starts moving it keeps moving in to you off the wicket. Walker is not an easy customer to get on top of early in your innings. His line is difficult to judge and for this reason John could be excused for letting the ball go.

Bevan Congdon came in and after he had been at the wicket for about half an hour I hit a ball firmly to Ian Redpath's left at extra cover. I played it, looked, and called 'yes'. There was no doubt as to the loudness of the call, and away I went for the single. It wasn't until I was two-thirds down the wicket that I realised that he wasn't coming. At that stage Bevan called 'No'. I said, 'Oh, you've got to come – ' I was dismayed and fully committed and Bevan of course was stranded. I think what probably happened was that even though he had been at the wicket for half an hour he didn't quite feel that he was up with the tempo of the game and the tenseness of the situation. Although it was my call I don't always believe you should go if the other batsman calls you – everyone has the right of refusal – but if you do refuse you must refuse immediately and so give the other batsman a chance to go back to his ground. On this occasion Bevan had watched the ball and not me and by the time he did say 'No' it was too late to do anything about it.

Bevan's run-out came at a vital stage and in restrospect I can say that if we hadn't won the match more attention would probably have been focused on this run out. It would certainly have assumed greater, perhaps even tragic, proportions. Fortunately, Brian Hastings came in and we put on 115 together and this was the deciding partnership.

During this partnership a regrettable and much publicised incident occurred. It was very near the end of the days' play and in fact about three overs only remained. Ashley Mallett was bowling and I was at the non-striker's end when Brian hit him over the top to the vacant wide mid-on position. As the ball was obviously going to the boundary I stood my ground and watched it. It clearly bounced inside the boundary by about six yards, and it cleared the fence with one bounce and ended up in the stand. A couple of elated, enthusiastic and, by that time of day, quite likely semi-intoxicated spectators signalled six. This was probably an involuntary action on their part. I turned to see Bob Monteith, the umpire, signalling six. As can quite often happen he'd lost sight of the ball in the crowd and was accepting the spectators' signal as being gospel. I said to him, 'Did you lose sight of that one, Bob?' 'Why, Why, Why?' he replied. I said, 'Well actually it clearly bounced inside the boundary.' He said, 'Oh, thanks, thanks very much.' He was about to signal four when Ian Chappell, who had sprinted up from slip, arrived on the scene. He was obviously in an emotional state. He began by suggesting that the umpire was blind and so forth and used rather foul language in doing so. I quietly went to say to Ian that it was okay, that things had been sorted out, that Bob was about to signal four, but before I got half way through this he blew his top completely and wasn't prepared to wait and listen to what I was trying to say. At this point he began abusing me, telling me to mind my own business and the language he used was as bad as you'd hear anywhere. It didn't happen just once; it was not as if it was just one sentence, for he carried it on, and on. I began to feel that he wanted to draw the incident out and I shrugged my shoulders in amazement and said nothing until he eventually trotted back to his position at slip. When I got down to the striker's end I went to say to Rod Marsh, 'Well, actually I was just trying to point out that it was a four. . .' but before I got half way through that Ian began abusing me again, telling me that he would see me later on etc. etc. At this point I walked away from the wicket but he carried on so I told him that until he stopped his rattling I wasn't interested in continuing the game. He ceased and the game carried on. Unfortunately for us Brian got himself out on the third to last ball of the day. He played an uncharacteristic shot trying to repeat his earlier shot off Mallett. Seeing that it was in the last over it didn't look too good, but of course the tension was great by that stage. Brian said to me later, 'I don't know why I did it, but I just did.' In one way that doesn't make a lot sense but in another it makes very good sense indeed.

The whole episode involving Chappell, myself and Bob Monteith was unedifying and unpleasant. If what had occurred had happened once only, and briefly, then one could have accepted it, but for it to have happened three times was too much. If a batsman plays and misses a few times then I don't mind a few words coming out; if the bowler lets go a choice word out of frustration then I can understand that – but when someone openly abuses you to your face and strings sentences together then I believe something should be done about it and this is why I asked for an apology.

We left the field in the reasonably happy position of being 177 for 4, and although we had six wickets in hand and only 51 runs to get we resisted the temptation to celebrate prematurely.

Jeremy Coney played coolly and well next morning and although he lost his wicket just before we got the required runs the match was virtually over by the time he left the crease. Ken Wadsworth was with me and drove Greg Chappell through the covers for four to bring up the winning runs.

A surprisingly large crowd had turned up that morning to watch us. One spectator was so eager not to miss any of the play that he stopped his car outside the main gates and rushed into the ground leaving his motor running. Everybody seemed highly delighted that we'd managed to beat Australia for the first time and the papers were full of reports of the victory. There is no doubt that this win did an enormous amount to foster interest in the game in New Zealand and this was the most satisfying aspect for all of us who had taken part.

From this point on relationships between the two teams became very tense and sour, and I have to admit that from here on all enjoyment went out of the series as far as I was concerned.

The next game on the Australians' itinerary was against my home side, Otago, at Dunedin. One understands that after having just completed such a torrid test match the Australians probably felt flat. One can also understand their wish to relax but nevertheless, no matter how unenthusiastic you might be about a game, I think you are obliged to put on a front and disguise your feelings, at the very least, and the Australians didn't do this against Otago.

Worcestershire county champions, 1974. From left to right: (standing) Keith Wilkinson, Ivan Johnson, Bob Lanchbury, Jim Cumbes, John Inchmore, Paul Pridgeon, Paul Roberts, John Parker, Ravi Senghera, Albert Shutt, Gordon Wilcock. (Seated) Rodney Cass, Brian Brain, Basil D'Oliveira, Ron Headley, Norman Gifford (captain), Alan Ormrod, Glenn Turner, Vanburn Holder and Jim Yardley

Khalid "Billy" Ibadulla, the Pakistan and Warwickshire cricketer who "found" Glenn Turner while coaching in New Zealand and encouraged him to go to England to be a professional cricketer

The only known photograph of Glenn Turner bowling —in a Sunday league match in England

The Otago match was undoubtedly the worst, most disheartening game of cricket I've ever played in. It was a travesty, and for much of the time an insult to the spectators and the Australians' opposition.

Conditions for the match were utterly miserable with a bitterly cold wind and occasional skiffs and showers of rain. The start was delayed until about ninety minutes before the scheduled close on the first day and conditions were barely fit for play when we did start, but fortunately for the Australians they batted first.

The Carisbrook wicket is noted these days as a wicket that takes considerable spin and this one looked as if it would be no exception. It was obvious that with the game reduced to virtually a two-day affair runs would have to be scored quickly if there was to be any hope of manufacturing a result or making an interesting match of it. People had come along expecting to see some of their leading players play sensibly and attractively but apart from Ian Davis's batting what they saw was mostly slogging and swiping.

The Australians declared at 158 for 6 and then Greg Chappell and Gary Gilmour ran through us and we were all out for 115. It was during our innings that the celebrated beer-can throwing episode occurred which sent a lot of people into a tizz. Play was held up for about five minutes while the cans were cleared from the field. For once the boys in section thirteen had overstepped the mark, being more intoxicated than usual. I think perhaps they were bored and irritated by events earlier in the day and this, along with the fact that you shouldn't give the big hitting Brian Andrews out lbw, was probably the reason for the boorish display.

After lunch on the final day Rod Marsh and Greg Chappell staged a deliberate go-slow and in an hour they scored 17 runs. Marsh's first scoring shot after lunch, when it came, was a nick wide of the 'keeper and down to fine leg for four. As he ran down the wicket he cursed at having scored some runs. Their defensive play was exaggerated, I think, because they thought we should not have been bowling our medium pacers but presenting them with runs so that they could put on another 100 or so in quick time before declaring. I could understand this but I think they failed to recognise the amount of turn there was in the wicket, and they also overestimated the ability of their opposition. It was my belief that if they'd left us 200 and five days to get the runs we wouldn't have managed it on that Carisbrook wicket. As it was we were left with two hours and twenty minutes to get exactly 200.

Stumps were drawn fifteen minutes early due to bad light when we were in the sorry position of being 39 for 6. It was only in the last half hour that they realised they had a real chance of winning and put fielders close to the bat to the bowling of Mallett.

On the conclusion of the match I felt that here was a perfect example of how the game is more important, is greater than the individual, and no one has the right to abuse the game the way it was abused during this contest.

From Christchurch we travelled to Auckland arriving there two days before the third and final test. We found the practice strips very wet and a look at the middle of Eden Park showed that it had also been affected quite noticeably by the weather. We were astonished at how wet it was with only two days to go before the start of the match. We thought that if the sun came out and providing the covers were left off, it just might dry out in time. But this was really more wishful thinking than anything else.

One gratifying feature was the amount of grass on the wicket. We'd all heard that during the Plunket Shield series Eden Park had gone back to the days where you expected shooters from the second day – these shooters are known as 'Eden Parkers'. In recent seasons the groundsman, Bob Beveridge, has worked very hard and has managed to get some grass to grow on the wicket, I believe mainly through plugging, and it has been playing very well, second only in quality to the Basin Reserve in Wellington. We found it difficult to understand, though, how so much moisture came to be in the wicket. We virtually prayed it would dry in the two days before the match. We all scurried out the next morning to see how it looked – it was bad news, it looked just as wet as the day before. In fact the ground was drier down both sides of the square then it was on the wicket. It seemed some water must have been put on deliberately. I guess the groundsman was probably concerned that the wicket might not last the distance so he decided to allow plenty of moisture on it at the start so that the grass would keep growing for as long as possible before dying off during the game. It seemed, though, they had either had too much rain in Auckland or he'd made a miscalculation, for the wicket was far too wet for the start of a game.

Once again, to our utter amazement, Bevan Congdon won the toss to make it two in a row. We claim that this must be, surely, a personal record for him. It looked as if we would have to put them in again, but as there were so many things to consider we held a real round table conference between Bevan, myself and Mark Burgess. Eden Park is Mark's home ground and he said he'd never seen a wicket on Eden Park that was quite as soft as this one was. You didn't need to be very clever to know that the ball was going to do some funny things. It was particularly soft at one end and I felt that it was sure to push up a piece unless it was just too wet for it to do even this. I felt that the wicket must get better during the first three days at any rate, so why not let them take the worst of it and hope that when we came to bat we'd get a very good score. I knew that the wicket was so wet that the top was going to lift off it at one end and this would mean that in our final innings we wouldn't want to be chasing too big a score – a wicket just can't repair itself once the top has been taken off it, and when the ball lands on the marks it can seam about alarmingly. By putting them in first we felt we would be giving ourselves our best chance of bowling them out for a low score. My vote went for what we call, in cricket, 'inserting'.

It was good to have Mark Burgess in the team. He is such a fine player and when available an automatic choice for current New Zealand sides, but he was to find out during this game that it doesn't pay to have too much of a break from cricket, wittingly or otherwise, for he was out of touch and couldn't

179

get going. Jeremy Coney, although he hardly deserved to be left out, had to stand down to make way for Mark's return.

Before the Australians went out to bat we knew that our bowlers would have to keep the ball right up to them and so make them play half forward, which would allow us to make the most of whatever the ball did off the wicket. Providing we kept the ball up it didn't seem likely that they would be able to score many runs and hopefully the ball would be seaming enough for us to get them out cheaply. We all knew that to bowl short at the Australian batsman would be disastrous. They play a lot of cricket on wickets which allow them to use the hook and the cut with some degree of safety, whereas New Zealand pitches just don't allow you to do this. This is one obvious reason why our batsmen are generally not very good hookers of the ball. We were criticised for not going for the hook or the cut more in this match, and while this argument has something going for it these critics tended to overlook the fact that the Australian bowling was praised throughout the series for its accuracy. The third test in Auckland was no exception: the Australian bowlers bowled far fewer loose deliveries than we did.

Keith Stackpole was out first ball to a chest-high full toss from Richard Hadlee. Full tosses are the best method I know of saving the wicket from wear. John Parker took a good catch at first slip and poor Keith was on his way to the pavilion again. Ian Chappell came in and immediately received a few nasty deliveries. Obviously this wicket was going to be one of those which forces the block-slog approach – a better way of describing this is to say that you try and keep out the good ones, and make a point of getting after anything that is loose, anything you think you might be able to get away for four. This became Chappell's tactics and when Richard Collinge dropped a couple short he whacked them in front of square for four. At the wet end the ball did really take off at times and it was close to being dangerous. It was so frustrating that our bowlers had one of those days when, though they knew they had to get the ball up, they kept dropping it so far short that the Australians were presented with runs even though wickets were falling regularly.

180

At lunch they were 93 for 5 wickets having scored at a rate of 5 an over. This was too fast under the conditions. I couldn't help feeling that the ideal arrangement would be for them to bat right through the day, scoring very few runs, while the wicket was being given the time to dry out. What was happening was that in between the outs they were getting enough loose bowling to keep the runs coming at a fast rate.

Doug Walters played one of his more valuable innings for Australia. He scored 104 on what amounted to a sticky wicket, and this was a tremendous performance even though our bowlers dished up more loose deliveries then you normally would have expected them to do. The Australians ended up with 221 and I thought, and so did most of the rest of our blokes, that we ought to have been able to bowl them out for not much more than 100.

Because the Australians had scored their runs so quickly they were able to bowl at us while the wicket was still lively and difficult. Before we went out to bat I thought to myself, 'Here we are again with another fight on our hands'. One thing about playing cricket for New Zealand; it builds intestinal fortitude. We are so often fighting from under that if you had the wrong sort of personality it could have a depressing effect. Opposition batsmen can occasionally afford to be cavalier, a pleasure we can seldom afford.

My approach when I went out to bat was to vary, I decided, according to the end I was at. At the wet end, where the ball had been standing up from a reasonably full length, I stood up more in my stance and tried to play more on top of the bounce. At the drier end, where the ball was doing less, I decided to allow the ball to come to me and wait and see how much it was going to swerve before committing myself to a shot. In other words I was going to play as late as possible.

The wicket played better for us than it did for them, so our own score was disappointing. Max Walker was the only Australian bowler really to make the ball stand up, and this only when he was bowling into the wet end.

Amazingly we were bowled out by Gary Gilmour who was bowling left arm over into the drier end. Gilmour is really a swing bowler who relies on movement in the air to defeat the batsman. He can be erratic at times, but he does swing it both ways and on his day he is a very good bowler.

It was silly and frustrating to be bowled out by swing and not seam or bounce on a wicket made for seamers. Many of our batsmen were very indiscreet and were caught in the slips region chasing wide deliveries.

At stumps we were 85 for 8. I was still there on 34, in a state of suspension, and somewhat aghast at having seen so many of our chaps come and go so quickly at the other end. One feels powerless in this situation: my main concern was to try to bat out the day and to hope like hell that on the following day a miracle would occur and I'd score lots of runs on a wicket that was playing perfectly.

Eighteen wickets had fallen in the day for only 306 runs so the match was virtually half over. Seven players had scored ducks, so seven chaps were sweating on a pair. The crowds who came along on the following two days, and there were between 30,000 and 34,000 on both days, were obviously going to see some action.

When we came out next morning Ashley Mallett came on immediately and he extracted more turn and bounce out of the wet end than I'd thought he would. I didn't last long; the miracle hadn't taken place. I played forward to Mallett and the ball gloved me and was caught round the corner on the leg side by Greg Chappell. This was virtually the end and we submitted for 112.

We knew then, at 109 behind, that we would have to bowl superbly if we were to have any chance. The wicket wasn't going to repair itself so any more than 300 as a target for us to chase in our final innings would likely be beyond us.

The first hour of the Australians' second innings put a seal on the game for them. Our bowling was again bad, we dragged the ball down short and they were able to score freely from cuts and hooks and pulls. Keith Stackpole finished the series in style, bagging a pair for the game as he got a nasty one which lifted sharply, gloved him and went to short forward leg where he was easily caught. We captured the second Australian wicket at 69 and the third at 118, but they continued on far too fluently to do our chances any good and finally reached 346. Here again they scored rapidly at a rate of about four and one half an over. Ian Redpath played a fine innings and batted right through the innings to be 159 not out. Although Hedley Howarth picked up three wickets, including that of Greg Chappell, he wasn't able to get the wicket we really wanted which was Redpath's. Redpath played Howarth very effectively by advancing down the wicket and smothering any ball pitched up to him. Batsmen seldom go down the wicket and play defensively, but this was what Redpath did and it was an excellent way, under the circumstances, of keeping his wicket intact.

We were determined to try to get the 456 required to win but on this wicket it seemed beyond us. Ian Chappell, because of the runs he had to play with, was going to be able to put fieldsmen up close to the bat when Ashley Mallett was bowling and as Mallett was going to get bounce and turn I decided I would have to use the block-slog approach when facing him. Anything he pitched up to me I was going to hit over the top.

Once again an unfortunate and unpalatable incident occurred early in my innings, just after Mallett came on to bowl. I pushed forward and the ball went from pad to forearm and was caught. The Australians appealed loudly which was justifiable as they were keen to have me out, and as they weren't sure what the ball had hit why not ask? But once again I was abused, and on this occasion I confess the abuse really did turn me on a bit. I was quite angry, because I had had enough during the series already and considered that things were already quite unpleasant enough without a repeat of the performance. There had been quite a lot of niggling right throughout the match, call it 'gamesmanship' or whatever you will. This is something you usually put up with, for if people want to act in a puerile manner that is up to them, but on this occasion when the direct abuse came I was quite incensed. My usual reaction to this kind of 'gamesmanship' is to treat it as being rather pathetic and usually it doesn't bother me, but on this occasion I was really angry and in some ways it helped my play. My senses had been sharpened and I was fiercely determined. One always tries to build into oneself the will to succeed, to find the fibre to drive oneself, and this is never easy, but when people do irritate me I find it helps me to find this fighting instinct.

At this stage Ian Chappell was in at a silly mid-off position, up very close for the pad-bat shot. The rest of the field was cover, extra cover and mid-off, and on the leg side an orthodox mid-on, a mid-wicket, a man on the sweep, a short forward leg and a man at leg gully. I decided there and then that when Ashley pitched the ball up it was going to go. Almost immediately he did pitch one up and I hit it very hard, though not with much loft on it, and it just cleared mid-off as it went very quickly to the boundary. A little lower and I could have been out. Then he tossed another up and I hit it over mid-on, then another over deep mid-wicket that nearly carried for six. He then dropped one short which I clipped past point for four more. Chappell altered his field slightly and put a man out fairly deep at mid-wicket, between mid-wicket and mid-on, but he left his man on the sweep behind square. Mid-off dropped deeper also so it meant that if the ball was on about off-stump I couldn't really hit it in the air as it could go to either of these two outfielders in front of the wicket. The only chance I had then of doing this was if he bowled one close in to my pads so that I could pick it up just in front of square. It must have been hard for Chappell to set a field for Mallett as I don't think he was really 'on' that day. I thought he should have been settling for line and length, for either he was trying to vary his bowling too much or he just couldn't put it where he wanted to. I was still able to hit him off the back foot through the covers and past point.

My only wish is that lunch hadn't come along for I had started to middle the ball and was even getting after the seamers as well. But as sometimes happens, when you have a break, I went cold on it and when I came out after lunch I began to struggle and found I'd lost my timing.

We lost our first wicket, that of John Parker, at 107 and from there on we lost wickets in embarrassingly quick succession. I was fourth out for 72 and we finally mustered only 158. It seemed a rather poor reply but I feel if we'd had 300 or slightly more to chase then we'd have got very close, but 456 was really out of reach.

The result was very disappointing for us for we had played well in Christchurch and, importantly, our bowlers had bowled so well there. There is no denying that our performance at Eden Park was bad for we batted in better conditions than the Australians. It would have been nice to have played this last match on a wicket as plumb as the one at the Basin Reserve had been.

When I finally left the ground at Auckland after having being dismissed in our second innings it was with enormous relief that the series had come to an end. There had been more tension in this series than any other in which I had played. The pressure is always on in test cricket but not the sort of pressure that had been on in this series. Also, two out of the three wickets we had played on had demanded a great deal of concentration as they were difficult to bat on. It was only during a period in my first innings at Wellington and in my second innings at Auckland that I felt that I was playing as well as I can play, so the series took more out of me as far as difficulty in making runs is concerned than I like.

Throughout this chapter I have tried to restrict myself to stating the facts only of the incidents as and when they occurred. I have made a particular point of not introducing any incidents other than those that have already been reported or were common knowledge.

By and large I am a great believer in the idea that things within the game should be dealt with by the governing bodies concerned. It is their responsibility to sort out problems that arise: I certainly do not believe that everything that happens on or off the field should become public property. This is why I have confined my remarks to the washing already hung out. Basically I felt strongly that some things needed to be said for the good of the game before all else, and if my remarks result in an overall tightening of the standard of conduct required of players on and off the field then it will have been worthwhile. I am sure that if each series were played in the way this one was I personally would not remain in the game very long.

For the Record

Details of Glenn Turner's test
and first-class cricket career
1964–1974

Glenn Turner's first-class career, season by season, tour by tour in New Zealand and for New Zealand Overseas

	Matches	Inn.	N.O.	H.S.	Agg.	Av.	50	100	Catches	Miscellaneous
1964–65 (N.Z.; P.S. and v Pak.)	6	10	1	28	126	14.0	0	0	5	Debut at age 17
1965–66 (N.Z.; P.S. and Pres. XI v M.C.C.)	6	11	4	95	330	47.1	3	0	0	95, 48* v CD; 55, 71* v C
1966–67 (N.Z.; P.S. and N.Z. U/23 v C.D.)	6	11	1	64	224	22.4	1	0	6	
1968–69 (N.Z.; P.S., Tests, S.I. v N.I., W.I.)	10	16	1	167	708	47.2	3	2	9	167 v W, 123 SI v WI
1969 (N.Z. in England)	12	22	3	124	644	33.9	4	1	14	124 v Mddx.
(N.Z. in India)	5	9	1	57	189	23.6	2	0	7	
(N.Z. in Pakistan)	2	4	0	110	269	67.2	2	1	4	71, 62 v Pres. XI; 110 v Pak.
1969–70 (N.Z. in Australia)	3	6	0	99	205	34.2	2	0	6	99, 67 v Tas.; pair v Vic.
(N.Z.: N.Z., N.Z. U/23, O. all v Aus.)	5	9	1	57	160	20.0	1	0	4	
1970–71 (N.Z.: P.S., N.Z. v Eng., S.I. v N.I.)	8	16	1	76	517	34.5	4	0	12	
(N.Z. v West Aus.)	1	1	0	8	8	8.0	0	0	0	101* v W
1971–72 (N.Z.: P.S.)	5	10	3	101*	424	60.6	2	1	7	Four double-centuries
(N.Z. in West Indies)	12	17	2	259	1284	85.6	3	4	14	132 v A; 131 v W
1972–73 (N.Z.: P.S. and N.Z. v Pak.)	8	14	1	132	644	49.5	1	2	7	1000 pre-June
1973 (N.Z. in England)	17	28	6	153*	1380	62.7	6	5	14	106* v Tas
1973–74 (N.Z. in Australia)	6	10	1	106*	265	29.4	0	1	3	101, 110* 2nd test
(N.Z.: N.Z. & O. v Aus.)	4	7	1	110*	449	74.8	2	2	2	
Total	116	201	27	259	7826	44.98	36	19	114	

B

Glenn Turner's test match analysis

		Matches	Inn.	N.O.	H.S.	Agg.	Av.	50	100	Catches	Miscellaneous
1968-69	(v W.I. in N.Z.)	3	6	0	74	183	30.5	1	0	4	Duck on debut
1969	(v Eng. in Eng.)	2	4	1	53	126	42.0	1	0	3	Batted thru inn. at Lord's – youngest.
1970-71	(v Ind. in Ind.)	3	6	1	57	105	21.0	1	0	3	
	(v Pak. in Pak.)	1	2	0	110	136	68.0	0	1	2	
	(v Eng. in N.Z.)	2	4	1	76	160	53.3	2	0	3	
1972	(v W.I. in W.I.)	5	8	1	259	672	96.0	2	2	5	two 200s; 387/1st wkt with Jarvis
1972-73	(v Pak. in N.Z.)	3	6	1	58	235	47.0	1	0	3	
1973	(v Eng. in Eng.)	3	5	0	81	116	23.2	1	0	1	
1973-74	(v Aus. in Aus.)	2	3	1	34	60	20.0	0	0	0	
	(v Aus. in N.Z.)	3	5	0	110*	403	100.7	2	2	2	101, 110* 2nd test
Total		27	49	6	259	2196	51.07	11	5	26	

C

Glenn Turner's analysis for Worcestershire and in England

		Matches	Inn.	N.O.	H.S.	Agg.	Av.	50	100	Catches	Miscellaneous
1967	(M.C.C. v Ox.U.; Worcs. v Pak.)	2	3	1	14	23	11.5	0	0	0	
1968	(C.C. and v Ox.U.)	25	44	3	106*	1182	28.8	8	1	17	106* v Mddx
1969	(C.C.; v W.I.; v Cam.U.)	11	19	4	66*	502	33.4	3	0	14	
1970	(C.C.; v Ox.U.)	25	46	7	154*	2379	61.0	9	10	25	10 centuries, Worc. record
1971	(C.C.; v Ox.U; v Pak.)	19	31	4	179	1126	41.7	6	2	21	179 v Pak.
1972	(C.C.; v Cam.U.)	21	38	4	170	1764	51.9	6	7	13	122, 128*; 156 all v Warks.
1973	(C.C.)	9	16	2	140	1036	74.0	6	4	6	76, 106* v Ex.; 140, 65 v Notts.
Total		112	197	25	179	8012	46.58	38	24	96	

D

Glenn Turner's analysis in limited-overs cricket in England

	Inn.	N.O.	H.S.	Agg.	Av.	50	100	Catches	Miscellaneous
1969–1973 Gillette Cup – 10 Matches	9	2	117*	405	57.9	0	3	1	
John Player Sunday League									
1969	6	0	52	113	18.8	1	0	1	
1970	15	0	66	411	27.4	3	0	13	
1971	11	1	43	308	30.8	0	0	7	
1972	15	1	121	642	45.8	3	2	2	2nd top agg; 4th av.
1973	8	1	129*	358	51.1	3	1	3	Top average
Sub-total	55	3	129*	1832	35.2	10	3	26	
Grand total, limited-overs competitions	64	5	129*	2237	37.9	10	6	27	

E

Details of test matches covered in the book, including Glenn Turner's own test record.

NEW ZEALAND v WEST INDIES 1968–69

1st test at Auckland: West Indies won by 5 wickets

New Zealand: 323 (Taylor 124, Congdon 85)
                and 297 for 8 dec. (Dowling 71, Pollard 51*)

West Indies: 276 (Carew 109, Nurse 95)
                and 348 for 5 (Nurse 168, Butcher 78*)
                Turner: 0 and 40

2nd test at Wellington: New Zealand won by 6 wickets

West Indies: 297 (Motz 6–69)
                and 148 (Yuile 3–25)

New Zealand: 282 (Turner 74, Edwards 5–84)
                and 166–4 (Hastings 62*)
                Turner: 74 and 1

3rd test at Christchurch: Drawn

West Indies: 417 (Nurse 258, Carew 91, Motz 5–113)

New Zealand: 217
                and 367 – 6 (Hastings 117*, Dowling 76)
                Turner: 30 and 38

Series drawn, one match each.

NEW ZEALAND v ENGLAND 1969

1st test at Lords: England won by 230 runs

England: 190 (Taylor 3 – 35)
                and 340 (Edrich 115)

New Zealand: 169 (Underwood 4 – 38)
           and 131 (Underwood 7 – 32)
           Turner: 5 and 43*

2nd test at Nottingham: Drawn
New Zealand: 294 (Hastings 83, Congdon 66)
           and 66 – 1
England: 451 – 8 dec. (Edrich 155, Sharpe 111)
           Turner was injured and did not play

3rd test at the Oval: England won by 8 wickets
New Zealand: 150 (Turner 53, Underwood 6 – 41)
           and 229 (Hastings 61, Underwood 6 – 60)
England: 242 (Edrich 68)
           and 138 – 2 (Sharpe 55*)
           Turner: 53 and 25

England won series by two matches to none.

NEW ZEALAND v INDIA 1969–70

1st test at Bombay: India won by 60 runs
India: 156
           and 260 (Pataudi — M.A. Khan 67)
New Zealand: 229 (Congdon 78)
           and 127 (Bedi 6 – 42)
           Turner: 24 and 5

2nd test at Nagpur: New Zealand won by 167 runs
New Zealand: 319 (Burgess 89)
           and 214 (Turner 57, Venkataraghavan 6 – 74)
India: 257 (Abid Ali 63)
           and 109 (Howarth 5 – 34)
           Turner: 2 and 57

3rd test at Hyderabad: Drawn
New Zealand: 181 (Murray 80, Prasanna 5 – 51)
           and 175 for 8 dec. (Dowling 60)

India: 89 (D. Hadlee 4 – 30)
                 and 76 – 7
                 Turner: 2 and 15*

Series drawn, one match each.

NEW ZEALAND v PAKISTAN 1969–70

1st test at Karachi: Drawn

Pakistan: 220
                 and 283 – 8 dec. (Younis 62)

New Zealand: 274 (Nazir 7 – 99)
                 and 112 – 5
                 Turner did not play

2nd test at Lahore: New Zealand won by 5 wickets

Pakistan: 114 (Pollard 3 – 27)
                 and 208 (Shafqat Rana 95)

New Zealand: 241 (Murray 90, Hastings 80*, Pervez 7 – 74)
                 and 82 – 5
                 Turner did not play

3rd test at Dacca: Drawn

New Zealand: 273 (Turner 110, Burgess 59, Intikhab 5 – 91)
                 and 200 (Burgess 119*, Intikhab 5 – 91)

Pakistan: 290 – 7 dec. (Asif 92)
                 and 51 – 4
                 Turner: 110 and 26

New Zealand won series by one match to none.

NEW ZEALAND v ENGLAND 1970–71

1st test at Christchurch: England won by 8 wickets

New Zealand: 65 (Underwood 6 – 12)
                 and 254 (Turner 76, Underwood 6 – 85)

England: 231 (D'Oliveira 100)
                 and 89 – 2
                 Turner: 11 and 76

195

2nd test at Auckland: Drawn

England: 321 (Knott 101, Lever 64, Cunis 6 – 76)
and 237 (Knott 96)

New Zealand: 313 – 7 dec. (Burgess 104, Turner 65, Underwood 5 – 108)
and 40 – 0
Turner: 65 and 8*

England won series by one match to none.

NEW ZEALAND v WEST INDIES 1971-72

1st test at Kingston: Drawn

West Indies: 508 – 4 dec. (Rowe 214, Fredericks 163)
and 218 – 3 dec. (Rowe 100*)

New Zealand: 386 (Turner 223*, Wadsworth 78)
and 236 – 6 (Burgess 101)
Turner 223* and 21

2nd test at Port of Spain: Drawn

New Zealand: 348 (Congdon 166*)
and 288 – 3 dec. (Turner 95, Congdon 82)

West Indies: 341 (C. Davis 90)
and 121 – 5
Turner: 2 and 95

3rd test at Bridgetown: Drawn

West Indies: 133 (Taylor 7 – 74)
and 564 – 8 (Davis 183, Sobers 142)

New Zealand: 422 (Congdon 126, Hastings 105)
Turner: 21

4th test at Georgetown: Drawn

West Indies: 365 – 7 dec. (Kallicharran 100*)
and 86 – 0

New Zealand: 543 – 3 dec (Turner 259, Jarvis 182)
Turner: 259

5th test at Port of Spain: Drawn

West Indies: 368 (Kallicharran 101)
and 194 (Taylor 5 – 41)

New Zealand: 162 (Inshan Ali 5 – 59)
and 253 – 7
Turner: 1 and 50

All matches drawn.

NEW ZEALAND v PAKISTAN 1972-73

1st test at Wellington: Drawn

Pakistan: 357 (Sadiq 166, Majid 79)
and 290 – 6 dec. (Majid 79)

New Zealand: 325 (Burgess 79, Hastings 72)
and 78 – 3
Turner 43 and 49*

2nd test at Dunedin: Pakistan won by an innings and 166 runs

Pakistan: 507 – 6 dec. (Mushtaq 201, Asif 175)

New Zealand: 156 (Intikhab 7 – 52)
and 185 (Pollard 61, Mushtaq 5 – 49)
Turner: 37 and 24

3rd test at Auckland: Drawn

Pakistan: 402 (Majid 110)
and 271

New Zealand: 402 (Hastings 110, Redmond 107, Collinge 68*,
Intikhab 6 – 127)
and 92 – 3 (Redmond 56)
Turner: 58 and 24

Pakistan won series one match to none.

NEW ZEALAND v ENGLAND 1973

1st test at Nottingham: England won by 38 runs

England: 250
and 325 – 8 dec. (Greig 139, Amiss 138*)

New Zealand: 97
and 440 (Congdon 176, Pollard 116)
Turner: 11 and 9

2nd test at Lords: Drawn

England: 253
and 463 – 8 dec. (Fletcher 178, Boycott 92)
New Zealand: 551 – 9 dec. (Congdon 175, Pollard 105* Burgess 105, Old 5 – 113)
Turner: 4

3rd test at Leeds: England won by an innings and 1 run

New Zealand: 276 (Burgess 87)
and 142 (Turner 81, Arnold 5 – 27)
England: 419 (Boycott 115, Fletcher 81)
Turner 81 and 11

England won series by two matches to none.

AUSTRALIA v NEW ZEALAND 1973–74 (in Australia)

1st test at Melbourne: Australia won by an innings and 25 runs

Australia: 462 – 8 dec. (Stackpole 122)
New Zealand: 237 (Wadsworth)
and 200
Turner: 6 and absent hurt

2nd test at Sydney: Drawn

New Zealand: 312 (Parker 108)
and 305 (Morrison 117, Hastings 83)
Australia: 162
and 30 – 2
Turner was injured and did not play

3rd test at Adelaide: Australia won by an innings and 57 runs

Australia: 477 (Marsh 132, Walters 94, O'Sullivan 5 – 148)

New Zealand: 218
and 202 (Congdon 71*, Dymock 5 – 58)
Turner: 20 and 34

Australia won series by two matches to none.

NEW ZEALAND v AUSTRALIA 1974 (in New Zealand)

1st test at Wellington: Drawn

Australia: 511 – 5 dec. (G. Chappell 247*, I. Chappell 145)
and 460 – 8 dec. (G. Chappell 133, I. Chappell 121)

New Zealand: 484 (Congdon 132, Hastings 101, Turner 79)
Turner: 79

2nd test at Christchurch: New Zealand won by 5 wickets

Australia: 223
and 259

New Zealand: 255 (Turner 101)
and 228 – 5 (Turner 110*)
Turner: 101 and 110*

(This is the first victory by New Zealand over Australia. Turner established a new New Zealand record by scoring a century in each innings.)

3rd test at Auckland: Australia won by 297 runs

Australia: 221 (Walters 104*)
and 346 (Redpath 159*)

New Zealand: 112 (Turner 41)
and 158 (Turner 72)
Turner: 41 and 72

Series drawn, one match each.